An Architectural
Guidebook to
the National Parks
California • Oregon • Washington

4 Oregon Caves Chateau, 1936

An Architectural Guidebook to the
NATIONAL PARKS
California • Oregon • Washington

Harvey H. Kaiser

GIBBS SMITH

Gibbs Smith, Publisher

Salt Lake City

Photographs and images courtesy of,
  BOR, 45, 47
  HABS/HAER, 2, 76, 98, 139,143, 154, 162, 258 (lower), 259, 261, 265, 266,
      267, 268
  National Archives, War Relocation Authority, 70–71
  National Park Service, 25, 29, 30, 31, 45, 47, 76, 77, 123, 131, 142 (upper),
      145, 152, 194, 197, 204, 205, 207, 212, 215, 225, 226, 233, 239, 244,
      248, 250 (upper), 252, 258, 259, 263
    Harpers Ferry Center, 19, 23, 258 (upper), 260
    Richard Frear, 19, 23
    Laura Soullière Harrison, 159, 160, 216, 217, 218, 228 (left)
    W. J. Meyer, 258 (lower), 259, 265, 266, 267, 268
    Ronald M. Mortimore, 258 (upper)
    Cecil W. Stoughton, 260
  Point Reyes National Seashore, 79
  Yale University Library, 32–33

First Edition
06 05 04 03 02   5 4 3 2 1

This book published by
Gibbs Smith, Publisher
P.O. Box 667
Layton, Utah 84041

Orders: (800) 748-5439
www.gibbs-smith.com

Project directed by Suzanne Gibbs Taylor
Edited and indexed by Linda Nimori
Maps created by Holly Venable
Designed and produced by J. Scott Knudsen, Park City, Utah

Printed in United States of America

Library of Congress Cataloging-in-Publication Data

Kaiser, Harvey H., 1936–
    Architectural guidebook to the national parks : California, Oregon,
    Washington / Harvey H. Kaiser.— 1st ed.
        p. cm.
    ISBN 1-58685-066-0
    1. Architecture—West (U.S.)—Guidebooks. 2. Historic buildings—West
(U.S.)—Guidebooks. 3. National parks and reserves—West
(U.S.)—Guidebooks. I. Title.
    NA725 .K349 2002
    720'.978—dc21
                              2001005088

Contents

Acknowledgements

This book evolved from years of appreciating the historic architecture in natural settings. We owe acknowledgements to many individuals who inspired the idea, provided helpful advice and comments, and encouraged a venture that had the possibility of becoming an overwhelming task. Many miles were covered and many people shared information and thoughts; a casual conversation with a park ranger or hotel desk clerk sometimes led the way to a place or setting that would have been missed without their patiently offered directions or advice. An apology is offered to those who, in my oversight, are not mentioned.

The publisher of Chronicle Books generously permitted the use of original material that appeared in *Landmarks in the Landscape*, published in 1997. Some text and photographs contained in that lengthier treatise on the historic architecture of the national parks of the West is reproduced here. The deft editing hand of Jane Taylor is again appreciated where material she touched is used once more.

The nascent notion of guidebooks for the traveler on the historic architecture of the National Park System was percolating when Gibbs Smith and Suzanne Taylor offered the opportunity to consider the concept for publication. Gibbs' publications of architectural guidebooks of American cities established his passion for historic preservation. I especially want to thank Suzanne Taylor for overseeing the process of keeping me on track and bringing together the book's editing and design.

Without the generous contribution of time and interest of the National Park Service staff, the book would still be an unrealized ambition. In the NPS Washington office, Randall Biallas, Chief Historical Architect, and Gordon Fairchild encouraged the book's concept and permitted access to a trove of invaluable material. Gordon patiently led me through the NPS database of classified structures, doing so with tolerance for frequent questions that formed the backbone of the buildings and structures contained here. In the

Harpers Ferry Center, Ed Zahniser was a guide generous with his observations, identifying resources useful in the book's research. Ed's vast knowledge of the parks was invaluable, and he often closed a gap in information that would have been an embarrassing omission. Thomas Durant at the Harpers Ferry Design Center once again provided invaluable help in locating historic material. We are immensely grateful for his patience, encyclopedic memory, and generosity.

I am especially indebted to Stephanie Toothman in the NPS Pacific Northwest for a review of text on parks in Oregon and Washington. She performed admirably on short notice, and her effort is gratefully acknowledged. Gordon Chappell in the Pacific Great Basin Support Office performed a similar task for parks in California. Their responses caught errors and omissions and corrected my novel grammar.

An acknowledgment is due the many people who participated in the Historic American Building Survey/Historic American Engineering Record. The HABS/HAER files accessible by Internet provided historical documents and carefully researched and artfully drawn renditions of many historic structures in the National Park System.

My indefatigable support team—Mike and Jeanne Adams of Fresno and Carmel, California—took time from busy schedules to check manuscript drafts for Yosemite and Sequoia/Kings Canyon. They visited both parks for updates on buildings, and their photographs and comments are appreciated.

Many colleagues and people interested in rustic design and historic preservation offered advice and accumulated wisdom on the subject. Of particular mention are Paul C. Soper Jr. and Peter Bohlin, both with outstanding design talent that includes portfolios of excellent designs. Their works express a keen sense of appropriateness of buildings in the natural setting and a genuine concern for historic preservation.

Finally, my gratitude to my wife Linda for her advice, her fine sense of use of language, and her support for this book.

The National Park System contains the scenic and historic treasures of our country. The natural beauty of the parks is profusely described in soaring phrases by outstanding writers, captured majestically in photographs and paintings, and listed and cross-tabulated in a host of travel guides. Why, then, a guidebook to architecture when the central purpose of the parks seems to be their natural resources?

Part of the answer is found in the organic act of 1916 founding the National Park Service, ". . . which purpose is to conserve the scenery and the natural and historic objects and the wild life therein and to provide for the enjoyment of the same in such a manner and by such means as will leave them unimpaired for the enjoyment of future generations." Because of the phrase "historic objects," many units of the National Park System are buildings, albeit often in sublime settings. In addition to recognizable national landmarks—the Statue of Liberty, the Washington Monument, and the Abraham Lincoln Birthplace—there is a collection of cultural resources in the National Park System that draw the visitor's attention. Presidents' homes, historic lodges and hotels, and National Park Service rustic cabins are abundant throughout the parks. Some historic structures are shadowed by interstate highways in downtown areas of the city while others are discovered after miles of mountain hiking.

Another part of the answer to "why an architectural guidebook" is that there is simply none available dedicated to that purpose. As an architect traveling the country I found myself agreeing with Wallace Stegner, when he said, "National Parks are the best idea we ever had." After standing awestruck at the first sight of Yosemite Valley or the Grand Canyon and exploring the natural wonders, I often silently congratulated the vision that preserved the unique "idea." It was after I turned my attention away from the main attraction and noticed buildings, not the honky-tonk or roadside tourist eyesores clustered at park entrances, but the buildings of form and materials strong enough to carry away as an image of a park that seemed to fit with the landscape. In addition to the national park great lodges—the Ahwahnee Hotel in Yosemite, the Glacier National Park lodges, and the Grand Canyon Lodge—there are modest wood-frame buildings commemorating great figures and moments in our country's history.

Fortune struck when Gibbs Smith asked me what I was interested in writing about—a rare invitation from a distinguished publisher of works about the American scene. Without a grain of understanding what challenges would follow, I answered, "A guidebook to the historic architecture of the national parks." Eventually, I came to have a shadow of what Meriwether Lewis and William Clark's astonishment at acceptance of Thomas Jefferson's instructions may have felt like. An initial round of research disclosed that there are more than 22,000 listings of classified structures catalogued by the National Park Service. The number of units in the National Park System was more than 380 in the summer of 2000 and the number grows each year.

A framework for the task began to take shape by organizing the research generally to follow National Park Service regions. Although this has varied in recent years, there is a reasonable organization by states and contiguous geographic areas to produce a series of guidebooks of similar length on the contiguous forty-eight states. Though an easterner by birth and residence, I chose the states bordering the Pacific Ocean for this book, which is the first in a series that will reach the regions and states bordering the Atlantic Ocean. Undaunted by the potential enormity of the task and with an architect's curiosity, a fully loaded camera bag, and a pocket full of road maps (and an Internet connection), I set out to visit, photograph, and research the western states of California, Oregon, and Washington.

The selection of national park units and buildings is the author's preference. There are thirty-seven units of the National Park System and three affiliated areas in the western states with structures listed in the National Park Service's list of classified structures. Scores of buildings in the "crown jewels" of Yosemite and Mount Rainier, and individual structures such as the Eugene O'Neill National Historic Site in Martinez, California, illustrate the range of possible entries in this book. While the choices may seem arbitrary (and may be amended in future editions), both interest as historic structures and accessibility influenced final selections. For example, the North Cascades National Park is a place of extraordinary scenic attractions but with few and difficult-to-reach historic structures, so it was not included.

With only one exception—Timberline Lodge—all buildings in this guidebook are in units of the National Park System. Exercising an author's discretion, I included the lodge because it is an extraordinary example of a historic structure. Visiting the lodge, located in Mount Hood National Forest and within reasonable driving distance from Portland, Oregon, is a rewarding experience.

The selection of images to accompany the text also represent difficult choices. Among the author's collection are thousands of slides, photographic prints, maps, and drawings. The Internet expands this reservoir of potential choices. Space limitations resulted in a sample of material that conveys the image of a place or information useful to the reader.

The architectural purist may question the place in this book of reconstructions such as Fort Vancouver in Vancouver, Washington, or Fort Clatsop in Astoria, Oregon. Each reconstruction's accuracy of replication was considered. The author chose reconstructed buildings that were close enough to the original to facilitate an understanding of architecture at the time of original construction.

Historic structures in the National Park System can be a personal discovery or a specific destination. Set in the scenic splendor of Yosemite Valley is a small chapel that may seem insignificant in comparison to the dramatic granite 3,000-foot face of El Capitan and diaphanous valley waterfalls tumbling 600 feet to the valley floor. The importance of this almost 125-year-old structure is its link to the history of settlement and the human experience in the valley. It also helps to relate the visitor to the scale of the natural environment described by Thomas Wolfe in *A Western Journal* as "a canyon cut a mile below by [a] great knife's blade."

In contrast, the diminutive Fort Clatsop reconstruction is a pilgrimage for Lewis and Clark aficionados. The western terminus of the Corps of Discovery's journey is an obligatory stop for retracing the epic journey that halted for three rain-sodden months in a fifty-foot-square log stockade.

Use of material from National Park Service publications is acknowledged with respect for thoroughness in research and skillful writing. The reader will note that there are personal observations scattered throughout the park and building descriptions. The technical descriptions of "saddle-notched logs and shake-shingled roofs" and documented building dimensions are balanced with an appreciation of settings, events, and personalities. Omitting the story of the "Pig War" would be an unforgivable omission when describing the American and English Camps' historic structures at San Juan Island National Historical Park. An insight into Eugene O'Neill's life enriches an understanding of his retreat in the hills east of San Francisco Bay.

Returning to a place never seems quite the same as the initial discovery, but the National Park Service's excellent stewardship of the nation's natural and cultural resources—evident through building repairs, relocations, and ongoing interpretation—makes each visit an exciting experience. For me, driving hundreds of miles from an airport or casually walking along San Francisco's bay from Fisherman's Wharf to the Golden Gate Bridge evokes the same feeling of returning to a familiar place of sublime beauty, enriched by an awareness of the structures that interpret its history.

The organization of this book is by states and then by individual parks. The twenty parks and Timberline Lodge described here—twelve in California, five in Oregon, and four in Washington—are difficult to see in a single journey. Better to plan in advance for different regions or serendipitous opportunities when combined with other travel plans.

Maps introducing each state show the general location of parks and nearby major cities. For each park there are travel directions and a brief background of the park's history as a general orientation to the significance of the historic structure(s). Parks with multiple buildings are described in a sequence that follows a driving tour and hiking access to remote locations. An invaluable resource for full enjoyment of a park is found in the National Park Service brochures available at each site. These handsomely illustrated and well-researched publications can guide a rewarding visit. For those with a deeper interest in the structures described here, visit the Historic American Building Survey/Historic Architecture and Engineering Record (HABS/HAER) at http://lcweb2.loc.gov. The thorough research and documentation in photographs, drawings, and text by teams of technicians can be inspected and downloaded.

The season of the year and weather can limit access to some areas, such as parts of Mount Rainier National Park and Crater Lake National Park. Plan for weather extremes: a sudden Fourth of July snowstorm at higher elevations or a baking in desert sun necessitates flexibility in plans, clothing, and equipment.

Days and hours of access, parking, and disabled accessibility can be checked by Internet reference to www.nps.gov. The National Park Service Website has a page for each park that unfolds with layers of information useful to the traveler.

The nomenclature of the National Park System is useful to sort out the variety of parks in the system. The diversity of parks is reflected in the variety of titles given to them. These include such designations as national park, national preserve, national monument, national memorial, national historic site, national seashore, and national battlefield park. Although some titles are self-explanatory, others have been used in many different ways. For example, the title "national monument" has been given to natural reservations, historic military fortifications, prehistoric ruins, fossil sites, and the Statue of Liberty.

In recent years, both Congress and the National Park Service have attempted to simplify the nomenclature and establish basic criteria for use of the different titles and additions to the National Park System. The nation's profound interest in protecting the natural and cultural resources has a suitable framework for protection that will undoubtedly expand the future number of parks. The following are definitions of the most common titles:

National Lakeshores and Seashores

Preserved shoreline areas and offshore islands, with a focus on preservation of natural values while at the same time providing water-oriented recreation.

National Historic Sites and National Historic Parks

Parks designated as national historic sites preserve places and commemorate persons, events, and activities important in the nation's history. National historical parks are commonly areas of greater physical extent and complexity than national historic sites.

National Memorial

Parks that are primarily commemorative. They need not be sites or structures historically associated with their subjects. For example, the home of Abraham Lincoln in Springfield, Illinois, is a national historic site, but the Lincoln Memorial in the District of Columbia is a national memorial.

National Monument

A national monument, usually smaller than a national park and lacking its diversity of attractions, is intended to preserve at least one nationally significant resource.

National Military Park, National Battlefield Park, National Battlefield Site, and National Battlefield

Areas associated with American military history.

National Park

Generally, national parks containing a variety of resources protected by large land or water areas.

National Parkways

Parks that include ribbons of land flanking roadways and offer an opportunity for driving through areas of scenic interest.

National Recreation Areas

Parks with lands and waters set aside for recreational use now includes major areas in urban centers. There are also national recreation areas outside the National Park System that are administered by the National Forest Service, U.S. Department of Agriculture.

National Rivers and Wild and Scenic Rivers

Parks that preserve ribbons of land bordering on free-flowing streams that have not been dammed, channelized, or otherwise altered. Besides preserving rivers in their natural states, these areas provide opportunities for outdoor activities.

National Scenic Trails

Generally, long-distance footpaths winding through areas of natural beauty.

Related Areas

Besides the National Park System, four groups of areas exist—Affiliated Areas, National Heritage Areas, the Wild and Scenic Rivers System, and the National Trails System—that are closely linked in importance and purpose to those areas managed by the National Park Service. These areas are not all units of the National Park System, yet they preserve important segments of the nation's heritage.

11 Sequoia and Kings Canyon National Parks

California

Lassen Volcanic NP

Sacramento

Point Reyes NS
John Muir NHS
Golden Gate NRA Fort Point NHS Yosemite NP
San Francisco Eugene O'Neill NHS
San Francisco Maritime NHP San Jose

Fresno
Kings Canyon NP
Sequoia NP Death Valley NP
Manzanar NHS

Los Angeles
Long Beach Anaheim
Santa Ana

Cabrillo NM San Diego

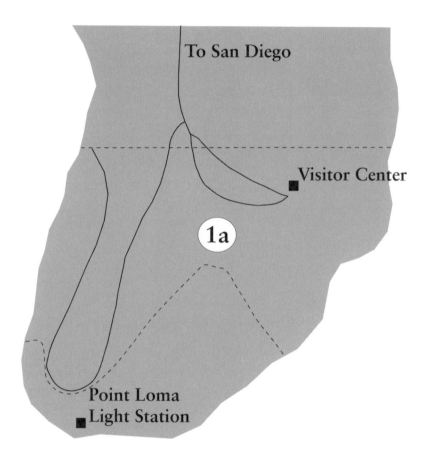

To San Diego

Visitor Center

1a

Point Loma
Light Station

1 Cabrillo National Monument

San Diego, San Diego County, California
www.nps.gov/cabr

Cabrillo National Monument is within the city of San Diego at the end of Point Loma. Driving from Interstate 5 or Interstate 8, take the California Highway 209 (Rosecrans Street) exit; turn right on Cañon Street; turn left onto Catalina Boulevard. Follow signs to the park.

■ "Nothing can be more beautiful that an entire apparatus for a fixed light of first order. It consists of a central bolt of refractors, forming a hollow cylinder six feet in diameter and thirty inches high; below it are six triangular rings of glass, forming by their union a hollow cage, composed of polished glass, ten feet high and six feet in diameter. I know of no other work more beautifully credible to the boldness, ardor, intelligence and zeal of the artist."

Alan Davidson, contemporary journalist

San Diego's 160-acre Cabrillo National Monument, established on October 14, 1913, celebrates the first landing of Europeans on what was later to become the West Coast of the United States. Sailing under the Spanish flag, Portuguese explorer Juan Rodríguez Cabrillo ventured up the West Coast of North America and arrived at San Diego Bay on September 28, 1542. Protecting San Diego Harbor on a headland reaching out into the Pacific Ocean, Point Loma was long occupied by the military and is the site of one of the last of the eight original West Coast lighthouses built in the 1850s.

JUAN RODRÍGUEZ CABRILLO

The 1542 expedition of Juan Rodríguez Cabrillo was a ten-month journey that took in more than eight hundred miles of coastline in Spain—and cost Cabrillo his life. Cabrillo arrived in the Americas around 1520. He was with Hernán Cortés in the conquest of Tenochtitlán, now Mexico City. Later, he joined Pedro de Alvarado in conquering and set-tling Guatemala. A successful landowner and shipbuilder, Cabrillo received command of the *San Salvador*, *Victoria*, and *San Miguel*, and, along with more than two hundred men, sailed north from Navidad, Mexico, and discovered the coast of New Spain. He left on June 27, 1542, and sixty-two days later arrived in present-day San Diego on the eve of the feast of St. Michael, the Archangel, where he "discovered a port, closed and very good which they named San Miguel." The expedi-tion remained there for six days and then continued north. Reports vary about an accident involving Cabrillo in November on one of the Channel Islands: whatever happened caused complications, and on January 3, 1543, Cabrillo died.

A fourteen-foot-high sandstone statue of Cabrillo in conquistador regalia, carved by Portuguese sculptor Alvaro DeBree in 1939, stands near the visitor center. Commissioned for the 1939 San Francisco World's Fair, the statue was delivered late and never displayed. A controversy over placing the statue in Oakland or San Diego was eventually resolved and the statue was brought to Point Loma in 1949. The sandstone statue of Cabrillo carved by DeBree was replaced by an exact replica in February 1988. The original had become cracked and weathered and is now in storage.

In 1602 Spanish explorer Sebastián Vizcaino visited San Diego Bay, changing its name from Cabrillo's "San Miguel" to San Diego. Nearly two centuries later, the Spaniards built a small fortification, Fort Guijarros, that occasionally fired shots at passing American ships. Point Loma became a station for processing whale oil after California gained statehood in 1850. The aggressive whaling campaign of the mid-nineteenth century almost wiped out the Pacific gray whale. Fortunately, the whales endured, and today the Whale Overlook, one hundred yards south of the Old Point Loma Lighthouse, provides superb views of the December-to-March whale migration.

1 Old Point Loma Lighthouse

The most prominent historic architecture in Cabrillo National Monument is the Old Point Loma Lighthouse. In the days of whaling, from 1855 to 1891, the lighthouse served as a beacon at the entrance to San Diego Bay. The location is 422 feet above sea level, overlooking the Bay and the Pacific Ocean. The site was selected by the U.S. Coastal Survey as one of a chain of navigational aids along the Pacific shore. Although visible for almost thirty miles in clear weather, the location had a serious flaw: coastal fog and low clouds often obscured the beacon. On March 23, 1891, the keeper, Robert Israel, extinguished the lamp for the last time. After thirty-six years, the old lighthouse was abandoned and a new light station went into operation at the bottom of the hill closer to sea level as a beacon for mariners.

The need for West Coast navigational aids came to Congress's attention in 1848. Locations were identified and officers of the U.S. Coastal Survey arrived at San Diego in 1851 to survey the harbor. Construction on the lighthouse started in 1854. The lantern itself—a Fresnel lens—arrived from Paris in August 1855. The "lighting up" ceremony took place on November 15, 1855.

The lighthouse structure is a whitewashed brick-and-sandstone two-story dwelling approximately twenty feet wide by thirty feet long. The Cape Cod–style keeper's house with a central lighthouse tower was the typical design for the original West Coast lighthouses. Gable-end chimneys symmetrically frame the building, although only the south chimney contains first- and second-floor fireplaces. The twenty-two-inch-thick sandstone outer walls rise from a basement level containing the 1,240-gallon cistern and the brick base of the thirty-eight-foot-high lighthouse tower. The original basement floor tiles may have come from Fort Guijarros. Emerging from the dwelling on a ten-foot-diameter, six-foot-high brick cylinder above the roof ridgeline, the glass-and-wood ribbed lantern rises another fifteen feet to the pinnacle. An entrance to the first floor from an exterior porch accesses the living and dining rooms and the tower. A wooden kitchen wing at the building's rear was removed sometime in the early 1900s and replaced with a stucco-exterior lean-to in the mid-1930s. The second floor is divided into two bedrooms and a "watcher's room" for the keeper and his two assistants. Tower access is up a spiral staircase that turns into a metal ladder, which opens onto the lantern floor.

The Point Loma Lighthouse houses a third-order Fresnel lens. Invented by French physicist Augustin-Jean Fresnel in 1822, the U.S. Lighthouse Board resisted using it until the 1850s. The Fresnel lens is like a glass barrel whose outer surface is made up of prisms and bull's-eyes. In a revolving or flashing light, the bull's-eyes are surrounded by curved concentric prisms, concentrating the light of a central lamp into several individual beams, radiating like the spokes of a wheel. In a fixed (or steady) light, the bull's-eyes become a continuous "lens belt," with the prisms parallel to it, producing an uninterrupted horizontal sheet of light. Fresnel lenses were classified in seven orders; generally, the larger a lens the greater its range.

Made in Paris, the Point Loma third-order lens stood over five feet high and three feet in diameter. In the center, a lamp with three circular wicks, one inside the other, produced a flame of 168 candlepower. The lamp used fish oil, sperm oil, colza oil (obtained from rapeseed from wild cabbage), lard oil, and kerosene. The lens magnified it to about 19,000 candlepower and was reported in 1862 as visible in clear weather from a mast height of twenty feet above the sea at a distance of twenty-eight miles.

Disuse of the lightouse and ravages of time, weather, and vandals brought about a recommendation in 1913 to tear it down. With a change of heart, the army made modest repairs in 1915. In an effort to stabilize the structure, the army encouraged soldiers and their families to live in it. In the 1920s the lighthouse was used briefly as a radio station. When the building transferred to the National Park Service in 1933, two years of careful reconstruction and repairs restored the lighthouse to what was believed to be the original condition. The monument was closed to the public during World

War II when the lighthouse served as a command post and radio station for part of the coast and harbor defense system. The military painted the lightouse olive green. In 1972 the park closed the tower to the public. In 1980 a major restoration project began that virtually rebuilt the lightouse from top to bottom. The majority of the work was completed by 1985. In 1995 the park added reproductions of furnishings from the 1870s and 1880s to reflect the lighthouse's active years. In 1959 and again in 1974, the monument was expanded, eventually reaching its present acreage.

Today the old Point Loma Lighthouse stands as a symbol of the first successful efforts to obtain aids to navigation for the West Coast. Overlooking busy San Diego harbor, the old lighthouse is a link with the past.

1 Old Point Loma Lighthouse; detail (p. 19)

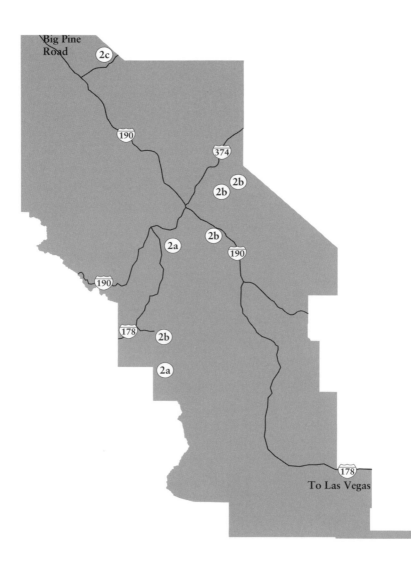

Big Pine
Road

2c

190

374

2b
2b

2b

2a

190

190

178

2b

2a

178

To Las Vegas

2 Death Valley National Park
Inyo County, California
www.nps.gov/deva

The park is transected by California Highway 190, connecting California Highway 395 paralleling the park on the west and with Nevada Highway 95 on the east. Nevada's connecting highways from north to south are at Scotty's Junction (State Route 267), Beatty (State Route 374), and Lathrop Wells (State Route 373). South of the park, Interstate 15 passes through Baker, California, on its way from Los Angeles to Las Vegas. State Route 127 travels north from Baker to Shoshone (State Route 178) and Death Valley Junction (Highway 190). The park is about a 2 ½-hour drive from the Las Vegas airport.

■ "Glassy heat waves dance above harsh, white salt, while dust devils gracefully twist across the desert floor, beyond the great mountains, upon whose sculpted rocks an incredible story of incalculable forces is written. This is Death Valley, an immense land that man has never been able to tame."

William D. Clark and Mary L. Van Camp: *Death Valley, The Story Behind the Scenery*, KC Publications

Death Valley is the hottest, driest, and lowest place in the contiguous United States, with fascinating geology, canyons and salt flats; desert surrounded by mountains; extremes of elevation (Badwater, 282 feet below sea level; Telescope Peak, 11,049 feet above sea level); and amazingly abundant flora, fauna, and wildlife.

The 3.336 million acres of Death Valley National Park, established as a national monument in 1933 and redesignated a national park in 1994, is 1½ times the size of Delaware. It was originally home to the Shoshone tribe. Speculation on the meaning of the local Timbisha Shoshone Indian tribe for Death Valley, *Tomesha,* is that it is a corrupted spelling of the tribal name. The tribe contends it more likely translates to "Red Earth," after the red or ochre earth found in the hills to the east of the present-day Furnace Creek facilities. It was in 1849 that Death Valley got its modern-day name. The Bennett-Arcane party of '49ers headed for California and left their guide for a "shortcut" that cost them their wagons, their oxen, and almost their lives. As the story goes, upon leaving the valley after crossing the Panamint Range and barely surviving the ordeal, one of the Arcane party bid the land farewell, saying, "Good-bye, Death Valley."

Gold prospectors left the valley frustrated and the borax miners of "Twenty Mule Team" fame found wealth above and below the ground. The valley has spawned legends of great silver- and-gold ore discoveries, lost mines, and rampant speculation. Visible evidences of the unsuccessful mining era are the ghost towns and abandoned mines and mills.

Within this unique combination of heat, landscape, history, and natural life, there are two resort hotels, ruins of gold and borate mines, and a remarkable historic structure called Scotty's Castle. Some of the sites are identifiable only by markers and accessible only by unpaved roads. The vast-ness of the park means you should locate the architectural sites beforehand.

Approaching from Los Angeles, one enters the park on California Highway 178 or 190 and passes near the Eureka Mine on Emigrant Canyon Road and Charcoal Kilns in Wildrose Canyon. Furnace Creek Visitor Center is a good starting point once you've entered the park. The Harmony Borax Works are also nearby. The Keane Wonder Mine is north of the visitor center off the Beatty cutoff, between California Highways 190 and 374. Scotty's Castle is in the northern part of the park, three miles northeast of Grapevine in Grapevine Canyon, and fifty-three miles north of the Furnace Creek Visitor Center.

2a Ghost Towns

The remains of once-thriving Wild West mining towns are scattered throughout Death Valley National Park or within a few miles of the park's boundaries. Discoveries of silver, gold, lead, and other minerals are memorialized in mines, dumps, tunnels, ruins, cabins, graves, and sometimes only markers within the park at Greenwater, Panamint City, Harrisburg, and Skidoo. The ruins at Rhyolite, a mining town of five to ten thousand people during its heyday from 1905 to 1911, are outside the east-side park boundary off Nevada Highway 374, four miles west of Beatty on U.S. Highway 95.

2b Mines, Mills, and Kilns

The Harmony Borax Works near Furnace Creek Ranch is a four-level ruin of buildings, machinery, tanks, piping, and waste tailings. A nearby town site contains remnants of buildings and trash dumps relating to the company settlement. The Works began to process borate ore in 1883 and closed five years later with the collapse of owner William Tell Coleman's financial empire. Later acquired and mined by the Pacific Coast Borax Company, the works inspired pitchman Stephen T. Mather (later to become the National Park Service's first director) to copyright the phrase "Twenty Mule Team" for the Pacific Coast Borax Company. The teams hauled the $36^1/_2$-ton loads of milled ore (borax) 165 miles to Mojave, a one-way trip of ten to twelve days.

The ruins of the Keane Wonder Mine mark the site of one of the most productive gold mines in the Death Valley area. The "Wonder" came from prospector John "Jack" Keane and his partner, a one-eyed Basque butcher named Domingo Etcharren, after their first strike in eight years of desert prospecting. They had been working on a particular ledge for several months, but were unsuccessful. Jack Keane, quite by accident, discovered an immense ledge of free-milling gold by the work site and named the claim the Keane Wonder mine. At the peak of production in the early 1900s, the site contained a stamp mill, a 4,700-foot-long aerial tramway system, boarding house, office, and family house. Working the mine in the summer temperatures of more than 120 degrees had its challenges—eating was difficult when utensils became too hot to handle.

A picturesque row of ten charcoal kilns is located in Wildrose Canyon on the western side of the park. Built in 1877 by George Hearst's Modock Consolidated Mining Company to produce charcoal for two silver-lead smelters in the Argus Range, twenty-five miles to the west, the kilns shut down in 1878 when the Argus mines' ore deteriorated in quality. The town of Wildrose, a now vanished temporary camp, housed about one hundred people, including forty woodcutters and associated workmen. The masonry beehive-shaped structures are approximately twenty-five feet tall and thirty feet in circumference. Each kiln held forty-two cords of pinyon pine logs and would, after burning for a week, produce two thousand bushels of charcoal. The kilns' durability is attributed to fine workmanship and short duration of use.

2c Death Valley Ranch (Scotty's Castle)

Death Valley Ranch (Scotty's Castle) rises out of the desert like a Castilian ranch in the northeast corner of Death Valley National Park. Built during the 1920s by a Chicago insurance executive as a vacation retreat, the Spanish Mediterranean–style multibuilding complex is in good condition. Scotty's Castle is a historic museum with costumed living history tours, technology tours into the basement area, a bookstore, and a fast-food restaurant.

WALTER "SCOTTY" SCOTT

Walter Scott, popularly known as "Death Valley Scotty," was born in 1872 in Kentucky, the son of a horse breeder and trainer. As a boy he ran away from home to join his brother on a ranch in Nevada. He worked at different jobs in the area, including jobs in Death Valley on twenty-mule teams hauling borax. In 1890 a talent scout for Buffalo Bill's Wild West Show discovered him, and he began working as a roper, shooter, and trick rider. After twelve years with the show, he began seeking investors for nonexistent gold-mining operations. In 1904 he met Albert Johnson, a Chicago insurance executive. The two men became friends and business associates, although Johnson's only profit in the venture was entertainment from Scott's stories, as well as a remarkable improvement in his health after several visits to Death Valley. By 1915 Johnson had decided to spend a portion of each winter in the desert, and his wife, Bessie, wanted a proper home suitable for entertaining.

2c Death Valley Ranch (Scotty's Castle)

Construction of Death Valley Ranch began in 1922. Throughout the ten-year construction period, Scott referred to the building as "my castle," and it soon became known as "Scotty's Castle." By 1925 the ranch consisted of a large main building containing the Johnsons' apartment, a garage with an attached shed, a chicken coop, and a bunkhouse. In 1926 Los Angeles architect Charles Alexander MacNeilledge was hired to redesign the main house, including many of its furnishings and ornaments. His work continued until he was fired at the end of the construction period. When work ceased in 1931, the complex contained more than 31,000 square feet of floor space. Ties from an abandoned railroad fueled the fourteen fireplaces. In addition to the castle and annex, the complex includes stables, a guest house (called the hacienda), the cookhouse, the gas tank house and service station, the powerhouse, the chimes tower, the gatehouse apartment, the long shed bunkhouse (today an employee residence), Scotty's original castle, and an unfinished swimming pool.

**2c Death Valley Ranch (Scotty's Castle),
adobe wall with shield (above, facing); shield (p. 25)**

Three miles east of Grapevine along the Scotty Castle Road, the apparition of a Spanish Mediterranean hacienda, complete with red-tile roof and towers, rises out of the desert. Through the entrance gate and past the incomplete swimming pool, the visitor historically arrived at an entry plaza. The main house is to the left, the annex to the right; the wrought-iron-decorated east gate with intricately carved stone abutments is aligned with the freestanding clock tower.

The two-story-high castle buildings are predominately reinforced-concrete construction with structural tiles and brick; stucco walls and red Mission-style roof tiles complete the Spanish Mediterranean exteriors. The castle is adorned with imported antiques, handcrafted furniture, European artwork, tile flooring throughout, wrought-iron hardware, and exposed structure with hand-adze marking, ceiling planking, and redwood trim. Many of the custom-designed furnishings and fixtures reflect a desert motif by incorporating the images of regional fauna and flora in their design. The hacienda, stable, cookhouse, and other support buildings maintain the same motif of Spanish Mediterranean character with stucco walls and red Mission-style roofs.

The main house contains a two-story living hall with an elegant central chandelier soaring up to the redwood-planked ceiling. At opposite ends of the approximately 31-by-32-foot-square room is a fireplace and grotto fountain framed in decorative tiles, respectively. A second-floor gallery surrounds the room. On the north wall of the living hall, the large door of redwood with elaborate wrought-iron hardware opens onto the 116-by-24-foot patio extending the full length of the building. Other rooms on the first floor are Scotty's bedroom, the lower music room, solarium, dining room, kitchen, and porches. The main house's second floor contains the Johnsons' living quarters, a guest suite, a verandah, and stairs to the tower mounted with a weather vane depicting a prospector and mule.

The annex's first floor contains an office and apartment, enclosed patio, and kitchen. The second floor contains two guest bedrooms with random-pattern tile flooring, an upper music room, an "Italian Room" with intricately patterned tile flooring, and a separate open-air lanai. The music room is enriched with a custom-built theater organ, elaborately carved arched redwood roof trusses, and Spanish Gothic–inspired woodwork details. An internal spiral staircase provides access to the three-story Moorish tower.

The Johnsons died without heirs in the 1940s and willed the castle to a charitable organization called the Gospel Foundation. The foundation mainly offered guided tours through Scotty's Castle, rented rooms on the complex, and also took care of Scotty until his death in 1954. The foundation sold the property to the National Park Service in 1970.

3 Eugene and Carlotta O'Neill at home

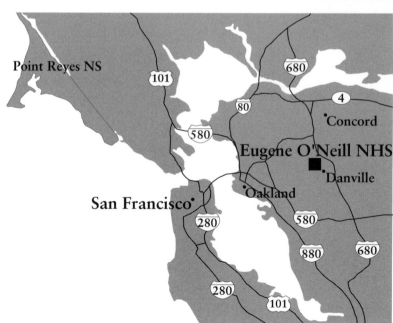

Point Reyes NS

101

680

80

4

Concord

580

Eugene O'Neill NHS

San Francisco

Oakland

Danville

280

580

280

880

680

101

3 Eugene O'Neill National Historic Site
Danville, Contra Costa County, California
www.nps.gov/euon

The Eugene O'Neill National Historic Site is located in Danville, California, twenty-six miles east of San Francisco in the San Ramon Valley.

■ "I never had a home, never had a chance to establish roots. I grew up in hotels. . . . It's strange, but the time I spent at sea on a sailing ship was the only time I ever felt I had roots in any place."
Eugene O'Neill

Nobel Prize–and four-time Pulitzer Prize–winning playwright Eugene O'Neill built and lived in Tao House in the hills above Danville, California, from 1937 to 1944. The fourteen-acre National Historic Site was also designated a National Historic Landmark (1971). Visitors with a National Park Service reservation can view the house and landscaped grounds on a 1 ½-hour guided tour to learn the story of O'Neill and how he influenced the American theater.

In 1930 Sinclair Lewis defined Eugene O'Neill's place in American culture by saying: "[O'Neill] has nothing much in the American drama save to transform it utterly in ten or twelve years from a false world of neat and competent trickery to a world of splendor, fear, and greatness. . . ." By the time O'Neill came to California in 1936, thirty-five of his plays were being produced for the stage. Restless and rootless most of his life, the introspective playwright and his wife, Carlotta, were living in a San Francisco hotel in early 1937: "No roots. No home," she wrote as they searched for a place to live.

EUGENE O'NEILL

Until he came to Tao House in Danville, California, America's greatest playwright had been a wanderer. Eugene O'Neill was born in New York City on October 16, 1888, the son of a touring actor, James O'Neill. The young O'Neill spent his infancy in hotel rooms and the wings of theatres. As he grew older, Eugene was sent to Catholic boarding schools and to Princeton University. Disappointed by his father's repeated performances of the melodrama *The Count of Monte Cristo,* and shocked by his discovery that his mother was addicted to morphine, he ran from them. At twenty-four, after itinerant years as a seaman, heavy drinker, and derelict, O'Neill began writing plays while recovering from tuberculosis. His one-act *Bound East for Cardiff* was produced in 1916 by the experimental Provincetown Players, who also staged his other early plays.

O'Neill quickly developed a reputation as America's most exciting dramatist. Often writing about tortured family relationships and the conflict between idealism and materialism, he taxed actors and scenic designers by the demands of his imagination, but he was no less demanding of himself. To O'Neill, writing was everything. He believed that the theater should be taken as serious art rather than pleasant diversion. He wanted to pull in his audiences, make demands on them, and commit them to the experience. Enormously prolific, O'Neill wrote nearly sixty plays in a career spanning three decades. In 1920 he received the first of his four Pulitzer Prizes for the tragedy *Beyond the Horizon*, a play that combined the real and the poetic in a manner that Broadway playgoers had not seen before. The next year, the tragicomic *Anna Christie* won his second Pulitzer Prize. His third Pulitzer Prize was for *Strange Interlude* (1928). He received his fourth Pulitzer for *Long Day's Journey into Night*, considered his masterpiece and awarded posthumously following the New York premier in 1956. O'Neill was awarded the Nobel Prize for Literature in 1936, the first U.S. playwright so honored.

By 1936, with no clear idea of when or how it would be produced, O'Neill had begun work on a cycle of plays about the history of an Irish-American family in America. Ultimately eleven-plays-long in plan, its theme was announced in its title, *A Tale of Possessors, Self-dispossessed*. When writing it, he often had to work on several plays simultaneously, and he needed isolation so that his concentration would be continuous and undisturbed. While he was visiting Seattle, he was awarded the Nobel Prize.

The isolated 158-acre ranch in the San Ramon Valley east of San Francisco Bay attracted O'Neill and Carlotta with its privacy and climate. Using the Nobel Prize stipend, they purchased the ranch and built the Spanish Mission–style house set against the Las Trampas ridge at an elevation of seven hundred feet. Here, they planned what O'Neill came to call his "final harbor"—Tao House.

Surrounded by extensive landscaped grounds, the two-story structure with white adobe-like brick walls, verandahs, and a Mission-style roof belies the "pseudo-Chinese"–style interior. O'Neill's interest in Eastern thought and Carlotta's passion for Oriental art and décor inspired the name Tao House. An interior of deep blue ceilings and red doors, terra-cotta tile and black-stained wood floors, and a collection of fine Chinese furniture create a cool, dark atmosphere. Visitors to the house are often unsettled by the darkness from drawn shades that protected Carlotta's sensitivity to light.

Two of the rooms of Tao House are refurnished, and photographs in each room show the O'Neills at home. One of the rooms, known as "Rosie's Room," was built especially for the O'Neills' pea-green player piano with painted roses. A glimpse of the intensity of O'Neill's labor can be experienced by a visit to the playwright's second-floor study, which is entered through a sequence of three doors and a closet, sheltered by thick walls.

Working unchecked for days or even weeks at a stretch, O'Neill poured out his masterpieces. Carlotta remembered her husband emerging from his study red-eyed and gaunt after working on *Long Day's Journey into Night*. O'Neill called it "soul-grinding" work. He regarded these plays as his life achievement.

O'Neill's daily routine at Tao House varied. Relatives, friends, and theater colleagues frequently visited the home. O'Neill enjoyed gardening and attending football games, where he relished finding anonymity in the crowd. He also walked the grounds, swam in the pool, and devoted time to his dog Blemie, the O'Neills' beloved Dalmatian and something of a surrogate child for the couple. A tour of the grounds landscaped under Carlotta's supervision with an oriental influence reveals the swimming pool, with its original bathhouse, and Blemie's grave.

Sheltered by the Tao House solitude, O'Neill produced his autobiographical plays: *The Iceman Cometh*, *Hughie*, *A Moon for the Misbegotten*, and *Long Day's Journey into Night*. During his year there, he turned his back on the theatrical world, giving himself over to transforming his past into the plays that made him America's most awarded playwright. Wartime unavailability of staff and the inability of either of the O'Neills to drive forced them to leave the sanctuary. Suffering from a rare degenerative disease and unable to write, Eugene moved to Boston with his wife, where he died in a hotel room in 1953.

The National Park Service continues to improve the visitor experience at the Tao House and grounds through acquisition of Eugene or Carlotta O'Neill memorabilia and original furnishings or period replicas reflective of the house's character. Seismic retrofit in 2001 ensures the stability of the unreinforced masonry walls. O'Neill plays are produced every spring and fall in the restored historic barn, providing a West Coast connection with the resurgence of interest in O'Neill's plays on Broadway.

Few visitors can leave this quiet atmosphere without the desire to reach for a volume of O'Neill's plays or seek out listings of active productions. The memory of the isolated second-floor study and the playwright who created his works there recalls Sinclair Lewis's words, "life is something not to be neatly arranged in a study, but terrifying, magnificent and often quite horrible, a thing akin to a tornado, earthquake or a devastating fire."

Visits to the site are by appointment. For reservations, write Superintendent, Eugene O'Neill National Historic Site, P.O. Box 280, Danville, CA 94526, call (925) 838-0249, or e-mail at www.nps.gov/euon.

Fort Point
National Historic Site

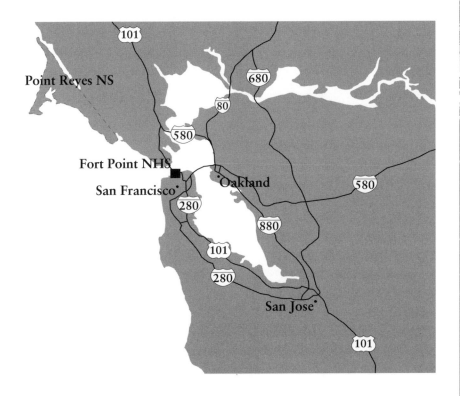

4 Fort Point, situated under a bridge support (above); section of the Golden Gate Bridge (facing)

4 Fort Point National Historic Site
San Francisco, San Francisco County, California
www.nps.gov/fopo

Fort Point National Historic Site is located beneath the south end of the Golden Gate Bridge in the Presidio of San Francisco. Parking at the fort is limited; driving access is from U.S. Highway 101 northbound before the bridge toll plaza, southbound after the toll plaza, turning left on Lincoln Avenue, and following this road along the shoreline to the fort. San Francisco MUNI buses #28 or #29 or Golden Gate Transit stop at the bridge toll plaza. From there, walk one-quarter mile down the hill to the fort.

■ "While the old fort has no military value now, it remains nevertheless a fine example of the mason's art. . . . It should be preserved and restored as a national monument."

Joseph Strauss, Golden Gate Bridge chief engineer

4 Fort Point, spanned by the Golden Gate Bridge

Fort Point National Historic Site, beneath the southern anchorage of the Golden Gate Bridge, was built to defend the entrance to San Francisco Bay. The fort, which would have been destroyed in the original plans for the bridge, was saved when designer Joseph Strauss reworked the design. The site, established on October 16, 1970, to protect this historic coastal defense fortification, is a fine example of one of about thirty brick-and-granite forts constructed as part of a national system of coastal defense between the end of the War of 1812 and the end of the Civil War.

The high cliff location at the narrowest part of the bay's entrance was the site of the Spanish Fort Castillo de San Joaquin. Built in 1794 the adobe structure was selected as the site for one of the forts to secure San Francisco Bay after California achieved statehood (1850). Alcatraz Island and Fort Mason also defended the bay, but Fort Point was the only West Coast part of the national "third system" of coastal forts. Influenced by Simon Barnard, a

French engineer brought to the United States, and Joseph Totten, later to become the chief engineer of the United States Army, the Army Corps of Engineers began construction of the fort in 1853. In 1854, Inspector General Joseph F. K. Mansfield declared "this point as the key to the whole Pacific coast . . . and it should receive untiring exertions." A crew of two hundred laborers, many of them unemployed gold miners, worked on the fort for eight years and rushed completion for the beginning of the Civil War.

COLONEL ALBERT SIDNEY JOHNSTON

In 1861, with the Civil War looming, Colonel Albert Sidney Johnston, commander of the department of the Pacific, prepared Bay Area defenses and ordered in the first troops to the fort. He sent 10,000 muskets and 150,000 cartridges of ammunition to Alcatraz Island, the primary Union defense post of the bay. Johnston deflated Confederate sympathizers' hopes that he would help them overtake the San Francisco Bay defenses and bring California into the Confederacy. He issued this fiery statement:

■ "I have heard foolish talk about an attempt to seize the strongholds of government under my charge. Knowing this, I have prepared for emergencies, and will defend the property of the United States with every resource at my command, and with the last drop of blood in my body. Tell that to our Southern friend!"

Kentucky-born Johnston later resigned his commission to join the Confederate Army; he was killed at the Battle of Shiloh in 1862.

Designed to mount 141 massive cannons, Fort Point was first garrisoned in February 1861 by Company I, Third U.S. Artillery Regiment. By October 1861 there were sixty-nine guns in and around the fort: 24-, 32-, and 42-pounders, and 8- and 10-inch Columbiads. After the war, the army installed powerful 10-inch Rodman guns in the lower casemates: these could fire a 128-pound shot more than two miles. At its greatest strength, the fort mounted 102 cannons. The fort had "hotshot" furnaces where iron cannonballs could be heated, loaded into a cannon, and fired at wooden ships to set them ablaze. Severe damage by more powerful rifled cannon on Fort Sumter in South Carolina and Fort Pulaski in Georgia made brick forts such as Fort Point obsolete. During the Civil War, as many as five hundred men from the Third U.S. Artillery, the Ninth U.S. Infantry, and the Eighth California Volunteer Infantry were garrisoned here. Enlisted men bunked twenty-four men to a casemate (vaulted rooms housing cannons) on the third tier; officers had single or double quarters one tier below.

The fort's plan called for three tiers of casemates and a barbette tier with additional guns and a sod covering to absorb the impact of enemy fire around an open-air, irregularly shaped quadrangle. Enlisted men's and officers' quarters, mess halls, and offices were located on each of the three tiers. The only entrance was a sally port with massive twin-leaved, studded doors. The lighthouse—the third built at the site—was used from 1864 until 1934, when the foundation for the Golden Gate Bridge obscured the beacon, rendering it obsolete.

Plans for the massive brick-and-granite structure with seven-foot-thick walls specified that the lowest tier of artillery be as close to water level as possible so cannonballs could ricochet across the water's surface to hit enemy ships at the waterline. Workers blasted the ninety-foot cliff down to fifteen feet above sea level. Because the fort was initially designed as a granite structure, granite was imported from as far away as China before engineers gave up on the idea of stone walls. Some eight million bricks were made in a brickyard nearby. Completed in 1869 the fifteen-thousand-foot seawall made of bricks fitted together and sealed with lead strips protected the fort from the San Francisco Bay's surging currents. For years, fishermen dug out the lead for use as sinkers on their lines. After more than one hundred years of being pounded by the powerful waves, it began to give way in 1980. The National Park Service rebuilt the wall and placed boulders at the seawall's base to deflect the force of the waves.

Although occupied by Union forces throughout the Civil War, the fort never fired a shot at an enemy. In 1892 the army began constructing the new Endicott System concrete fortifications armed with steel breech-loading guns.

4 Fort Point, anchored by the Golden Gate Bridge (above); gun mount (facing)

Within eight years, all 102 of the smooth-bore cannons at Fort Point had been dismounted and sold for scrap. The fort, moderately damaged in the 1906 earthquake, was used over the next four decades for barracks, training, and storage. Between 1933 and 1937 the fort was used as a base of operations for the construction of the Golden Gate Bridge. Soldiers from the Sixth U.S. Coast Artillery were stationed at the fort during World War II to man searchlights and rapid-fire cannons as part of the protection of a submarine net strung across the San Francisco Bay entrance.

A pleasant surprise is in store for the visitor who climbs to the bastion's roof. Braced against the blowing ocean winds, one can see the sweeping panorama unfold: the Pacific Ocean to the west, the headlands of Marin County to the north, San Francisco and the bay to the east. Ships and boats are often seen passing beneath the Golden Gate Bridge. The dramatic location of Fort Point under the Golden Gate Bridge's soaring steel arches attests to the capability of engineer's skills—for war and peace. Demonstrations by period-uniformed staff and a self-guided tour reveal the massive construction layered tier upon tier. Separated from the outside world by the sally gate and massive walls, the casemate's arched openings and silent cannons echo the generations of soldiers who were positioned in this coastal defense garrison.

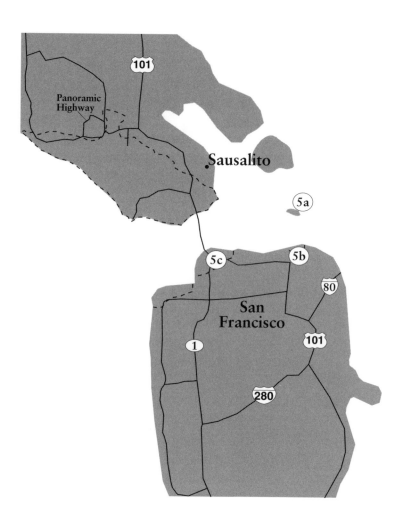

101

Panoramic
Highway

•Sausalito

5a

5c 5b

80

San
Francisco

1 101

280

5 Golden Gate National Recreation Area

Marin, San Francisco, and San Mateo Counties, California

www.nps.gov/goga

The San Francisco part of Golden Gate National Recreation Area stretches along several miles of San Francisco Bay's south shoreline from Fisherman's Wharf to Fort Point beneath the south anchorage of the Golden Gate Bridge. The walk past Aquatic Park through Fort Mason and the Presidio to Fort Point is one of the great urban walking trails of America. The area can be reached by car, although traffic is sometimes heavy—public transportation is recommended. San Francisco's Municipal Railway (MUNI) provides transportation to most sites. MUNI bus lines, Metro lines, and the Hyde Street and Mason Street cable car lines provide the most frequent service. The Blue & Gold Fleet ferries provide transportation to Alcatraz.

Golden Gate National Recreation Area (GGNRA) is a park of 75,000 acres that spreads across Marin, San Francisco, and San Mateo Counties. Located where the Pacific Ocean meets San Francisco Bay, it is one of the largest urban parks in the world—2½ times the size of San Francisco—embracing federal, public, and private lands. The Golden Gate Bridge is the link to cooperative solutions to protecting a spectacular blend of natural beauty, historic features, and urban development. Locations with historic structures are Alcatraz Island, Fort Mason, Fort Miley, Fort Funston, Sutro Area, Muir Woods National Monument, and the Presidio. (See text descriptions of National Park System–designated sites Point Reyes National Seashore, Fort Point National Historic Site, and San Francisco Maritime National Historic Park.)

The Golden Gate National Recreation Area, established on October 27, 1972, is dedicated to the memory of its chief legislative champion, U.S. Congressman Philip Burton. Park headquarters are located at upper Fort Mason.

5a Alcatraz Island

Notorious in American culture as the legendary U.S. Bureau of Prisons maximum-security facility for hardened criminals from 1934 to 1963, the sandstone island dominates the entrance to San Francisco Bay. Curiously, European explorers missed the entrance to the bay until Spaniard Manuel Ayala entered by ship in 1775. Ayala named the island Isla de Los Alcatraces, probably after cormorants (*alcatraceo* in Spanish) roosting on its barren, rocky outcrops. The name was later modified to Alcatraz, which some argue refers to the brown pelicans common to the bay. Ayala's named island, what is now called Yerba Buena, was later switched on a map with Alcatraz.

Alcatraz has had a lengthy and often turbulent history. After California achieved statehood, the island was the site of Fortress Alcatraz, then became the Pacific Coast's first lighthouse (1854), a Civil War bastion, a military prison, a prison for Native Americans, and the infamous depression-era federal prison. Ten years after closing the prison, the island was opened to the public as the first unit of the Golden Gate National Recreation Area. Visitors can reach the island by daily ferry service from Pier 41 at Fisherman's Wharf in San Francisco.

Alcatraz's present condition results from one-and-a-half centuries of reshaping the island to improve defenses and ensure its isolation from within and without. When U.S. Army engineers designated Alcatraz as one of a "Triangle of Defense" system of forts protecting the bay, laborers set to blasting at the rock and building steep walls around the island. Eventually 111 smoothbore cannon were mounted behind the walls. The lighthouse was built in the late 1850s; the Citadel, built at the island's peak, was the final defense in case of attack. Completed in 1859, the penultimate fortress bricks were shipped from the mainland, the sandstone quarried on nearby Angel Island, and much of the granite imported from China. As the main Union stronghold, fortifications were added to everything, including the prison barracks. Concern that Confederate sympathizers would seize the fort inspired the addition of reinforcing gun platforms. The end of the Civil War marked

5a Alcatraz Island, with Angel Island in the background; detail (p. 45)

the end of Alcatraz as an effective harbor defense. A plan in 1870 to protect against long-range cannons further shaped the island with cuts into the cliffs and the erection of earthworks. At the same time, the south end of the island was leveled into a military parade ground. Prisoners did the bulk of the work, building new batteries and structures and filling in irregularities along the shoreline.

The shipment of a group of inmates to the island in 1859 began the island's role as a military prison. The population varied between military and civilian prisoners and provided imprisonment for Native Americans, including in 1895 a group of Hopis protesting land disputes and mandatory children's education programs. By 1907 the army finally acknowledged the end of the island was an ineffective defense site and redesignated it as "Pacific Branch, U.S. Military Prison, Alcatraz Island." A prison complex of concrete was added for fire protection in the wake of the post-1906 earthquake fires. An ambitious building project under the supervision of Major Reuben Turner produced the cellhouse complex that is the island's most memorable image. Army prisoners tore down the upper Citadel and constructed the complex with four cellblocks of six hundred cells, a kitchen, dining hall, hospital, recreation yard, and administrative offices. It was the largest reinforced concrete building in the world when completed in 1912.

In 1933 the army, recognizing the high cost of maintaining the military prison during the depression, along with negative publicity, closed Alcatraz and in 1934 the Federal Bureau of Prisons moved in. Always a costly facility to operate, Alcatraz was finally closed as a prison in 1963. In 1972 Alcatraz became part of the Golden Gate National Recreation Area.

A tour of the architectural sites on the island begins at the ferry wharf. The remains of the old military post, military prison, and the civilian prison, blended with ruins of the 1970s Native American occupation, are visible on a self-guided island tour. A switchback road constructed in 1853 leads from the wharf to the top of the island past fortifications, casements with embrasures, the guardhouse (1857), sally port, chapel, and the lighthouse tower (1854) to the infamous cellhouse. Visible from many vantage points is the San Francisco skyline, the bay, and the headlands spanned by the Golden Gate Bridge.

The National Park Service offers interpretation elements, including guided tours, prison exhibits, and occupation videos; a cellhouse audio tour is also available.

5b Fort Mason

Fort Mason, west of Fisherman's Wharf, Ghirardelli Square, and the San Francisco Maritime National Park (see text description), marks the eastern boundary of the Golden Gate National Recreation Area on San Francisco's northern edge. It is the site of Spanish earthwork gun batteries built in 1797, and the U.S. government established a military reservation of Point San Jose in 1850. The U.S. military moved in during the Civil War, naming the area Fort Mason in the 1880s, and built gun batteries, barracks, officers' quarters, and a parade ground. The hospital built in 1902 now houses headquarters for the Golden Gate National Recreation Area.

Pacific military activities during the Spanish-American War resulted in the army expanding Fort Mason as a shipping center for supplies to the Philippines, Guam, and Alaska, and the destruction of leased piers on the Embarcadero by the 1906 earthquake resulted in the creation of the military port. Land was filled and from 1912 to 1915 construction was completed on the Mission Revival–style army-supply center, including three large piers and warehouses. The chapel was added to the post in 1941.

5b Gun mount at Fort Mason (above); Fort Mason building (below)

By 1962 transport by air made Fort Mason obsolete, and it fell into disuse and disrepair. The Fort Mason Foundation was created in 1976 to convert the empty buildings into a cultural center. Fort Mason's important role during World War II and the Korean conflict as the embarkation point for troops and supplies shipped to the Pacific earned National Historic Landmark designation in 1985.

A great meadow, community gardens, fishing piers, and picnic areas are available for public use. Overlooking the bay, the former Civil War barracks now serve as the San Francisco International Hostel. The thirteen-acre Fort Mason Center, the former San Francisco Port of Embarkation, has become a national model for the conversion of military facilities to peacetime use. Nearly fifty resident cultural, media, and environmental organizations provide a broad range of activities for all interests. Building A houses Greens, a vegetarian restaurant operated by the San Francisco Zen Center. Building C houses the Museo ItaloAmericano and the San Francisco African American Historical and Cultural Society. Building D houses the Mexican Museum and the San Francisco Craft and Folk Art Museum. Building E houses the San Francisco Maritime National Historic Park Headquarters, its Historic Documents Department, and the National Maritime Museum Library.

5b Fort Mason buildings (above and facing); Fort Mason chapel (below)

5c The Presidio

The Presidio of San Francisco served as the home of the Native people (the Yelamu Ohlone tribe) for thousands of years, and as a military installation for more than two centuries, occupied by a succession of soldiers, settlers and their families sent by Spain (1776–1822), Mexico (1822–46), and the United States (1846–1994). Long considered a choice military assignment for its location near downtown San Francisco, spectacular views, beaches, miles of equestrian trails, golf courses, and spacious living quarters, the Presidio contains a rich collection of architectural styles. Building types range from elegant officers' quarters and barracks to large warehouses, administrative headquarters, air hangars, major medical facilities, and stables. The rich collection of structures illustrates specific building campaigns that assisted in the Presidio's growth into a significant western United States Army post. Deservedly, the Presidio was designated a National Historic Landmark District in 1962.

Designated for closure as a military installation in 1989, the Presidio became part of the GGNRA, as outlined in the 1972 enabling legislation, and the National Park Service assumed total jurisdiction over the ex-military post in 1994. Coveted as a development site, the 1,480-acre tract of land contains a veritable "museum" of seacoast fortifications, a national cemetery, a historic airfield, planted forest, beaches and coastal bluffs, and miles of hiking and biking trails. Support for planning the future of the Presidio came from many sources, including the Golden Gate National Park Association (GGNPA), the park's nonprofit support organization.

The 1993 GGNRA Plan called for a great urban park, "a global center for exchanging ideas on critical environmental and societal challenges. . . . An environmental laboratory, a major focus of research and learning, and a demonstration area for ways to improve the quality of life." Implementation of the plan and stewardship of the Presidio's cultural landscapes, 474 historic buildings, and archeological sites are under the joint management of the National Park Service and the Presidio Trust, an executive agency of the U.S. government created in 1996. The Trust's enabling legislation mandates reversion of the Presidio to the Defense Department if the former army post is not self-sufficient by 2013.

The Presidio's historic structures illustrate the various army building programs to establish a permanent presence, with each successive campaign producing larger, grander, and more expensive buildings. There is a tremendous range of building types and styles at the Presidio, although buildings often evade strict stylistic definitions. Different architectural elements were often intermingled with the less elaborate interpretations of civilian versions, resulting in eclectic styles. To complement building development, the army also began a large-scale landscaping effort. By the 1890s tens of thousands of trees were planted along the ridges and perimeter in an effort to reduce soil erosion, provide windbreaks, and create the illusion of a larger, more impressive post.

BUFFALO SOLDIERS AT THE PRESIDIO

Among the gravesites and markers of the Presidio's San Francisco National Military Cemetery are 450 headstones of African American soldiers of the Ninth and Tenth Cavalry and the Twenty-fourth and Twenty-fifth Infantry. These are a legacy of the "Buffalo Soldier" regiments formed by Congress in 1866. Intended to help rebuild the country and to patrol the western frontier, six African American regiments of about one thousand soldiers each were reformed into two infantry and two cavalry regiments in 1869. According to legend, Native Americans called the black cavalry troops "buffalo soldiers" because their dark curly hair resembled a buffalo's coat. The name was accepted with pride and adopted by the infantry units.

Companies from all four regiments reported to the Presidio in 1899 on their way to the Philippines. Returning through the Presidio in 1902, four troops of the Ninth Cavalry remained until 1904. During this period, Ninth Cavalry soldiers served as the official presidential escort of honor for Theodore Roosevelt when he visited San Francisco in 1903, and as the safekeepers of Yosemite and Sequoia National Parks before there was a national park system. This was the first time that African American troops were given this honored role.

A visitor can trace the post's many layers of history, with Greek Revival and Italianate styles alongside Colonial Revival, and Mission Revival found in modern utilitarian buildings. Typically, the army put more design and construction effort into the high-profile buildings, such as the generals' quarters, headquarters offices, chapels, and officer housing, rather than in more utilitarian buildings such as powerhouses, storage facilities, garages, warehouses, and fortifications.

Many Presidio buildings were based on standard plans dispatched from the Army Quartermaster's Office in Washington, D.C. The early buildings, illustrated by the Cavalry Barracks (1862), were dressed in Italianate and Greek Revival–style details, but were later made less recognizable by stripping away the brackets, cupolas, and porches, and modifying them to resemble Mission style. Some 1880s Victorian-era officers' quarters (Building 59) built in Queen Anne style were followed by similar structures in the 1890s for the commanding officers' quarters and portions of Letterman Hospital.

Fort Winfield Scott, constructed as the new headquarters for the coast artillery defense, was the first Presidio building project in the Mission Revival style. In response to the success and acceptance of the orderly appearance of Fort Scott, new construction on the post adopted the style. White stucco walls and Mission-style red-tile roofs became the common architectural vocabulary. Buildings in the post–World War II era adopted the severity of Modern architecture, seen in the multiunit housing and the 1950s addition to the Public Health Service Hospital at the Presidio's south and west corners.

A walking or driving tour of the Presidio might begin at the William Penn Mott Jr. Visitor Center off Route 101 (Doyle Drive) in the center of the post near the parade grounds. Selected buildings of interest near the Lombard Street gate are the twelve historic Letterman Hospital buildings at the Thoreau Center for Sustainability near the Lombard Gate (1896); two wood-frame buildings behind the museum used as relief shacks to house homeless people after the 1906 earthquake; and the Post Chapel. The Officers' Quarters in the east housing area offer a variety of stylistic examples. The Officer's Club is a lesson in the Presidio's history: an adobe structure built in the 1820s, rebuilt by the Americans in 1847, remodeled in the Spanish Mission style in 1934, and then added to again in 1973. The building contains fourteen-foot-high adobe walls. There are two Peruvian, Fremont spiked cannons in front of the Quarters, originally from Castillo de

San Joaquin, one hundred or more years old when brought to the Presidio in the 1790s.

Crissy Field along the bay was filled for the Panama Pacific International Exposition of 1915 and later converted into an airfield whose utilitarian hangars are still prominent. Through a joint effort of the National Park Service and the Golden Gate National Parks Association, a $34.4 million restoration project reclaimed Crissy Field as a shoreline park. Crissy Field Center, located in Building 603 on the corner of Mason and Halleck Streets was built in 1939 and first used as an army commissary, later as a film and photo lab. The Center opened in 2001 and now provides mulitcultural environmental programming, community outreach, and education programs.

A circular route from Crissy Field leads to the south and west sides of the post, crosses Route 1, and passes other examples of a variety of architectural styles, seen in the Presidio Stables, Cavalry Barracks, and officers' houses in Fort Winfield Scott. At the northwest corner of the post are remnants of the fortifications built to protect the entrance to San Francisco Bay after Fort Point became obsolete (Batteries Boutelle, Cranston, Godfrey, and Miller). The walkway to Fort Point is accessed through the tunnel under the Golden Gate Bridge toll plaza.

6 John Muir House (above); Martinez Adobe, detail (facing)

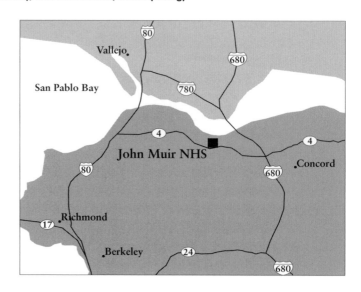

6 John Muir National Historic Site
Martinez, Contra Costa County, California
www.nps.gov/jomu

The John Muir National Historic Site is located in the San Francisco metropolitan area on the east bay in Martinez at the intersection of John Muir Parkway, Highway 4, and Alhambra Avenue. From Interstate 80, exit at Highway 4 and proceed eastbound toward Stockton and Martinez.

■ "Wildness is a necessity. Mountains and parks and reservations are useful not only as fountains of timber and irrigating rivers, but as fountains of life."

John Muir, *Our National Parks*

The John Muir National Historic Site of 334 acres contains the Muir House, orchards, outbuildings, and the two-story Monterey-style Martinez Adobe. The park, established in 1964, is a remnant of the original Martinez 17,000-acre grant and was built by the eponymous Don Vincente Martinez of Martinez. Muir's 8½-acre estate remains as it was when the conservationist lived and worked here from 1890 until his death in 1914. The National Park Service restored and continues to add furnishings and exhibits to the Muir and Martinez Houses.

The Victorian Italianate–style John Muir house in the Alhambra Valley in Martinez, California, presents a contrast between the cultivated, domestic grandeur of a fourteen-room mansion and the image of the outdoorsman who

6 Martinez Adobe

reveled in sleeping out-of-doors, trekking across his beloved Sierra Nevada, and extolling the virtues of wilderness preservation. Exploring wild nature's meaning, Muir came to California and met and married Louie Strentzel. In 1880, the Muirs moved into a small Dutch Colonial house on the Dr. John Strentzel family fruit ranch a mile away from the family house. Muir took up fruit ranching, prospered, and moved into the family house after the death of Dr. Strentzel in 1890. Financially independent after his ten-year partnership with his father-in-law, Muir relinquished day-to-day management of the fruit ranch in 1890 and devoted the rest of his life to the defense of the environment.

Muir returned home periodically from travels that spanned around the globe from Alaska to Africa, but concentrated mainly in the nearby Sierras. He was a pioneer spokesperson for the national parks, trekking thousands of miles and publicizing little-known wonders. Muir regarded wilderness as an object to be venerated, a restorative for modern man: "Thousands of tired, nerve-shaken, over-civilized people are beginning to find out that going to the mountains is going home; that wildness is a necessity; and that the mountain parks and reservations are useful not only as fountains of timber and irrigating rivers, but as fountains of life." He published more than three hundred articles in important American magazines and newspapers to publicize the conservation ethic. Muir was one of the founders of the Sierra Club in 1892 and served as its president until his death. His books were first published in 1894 and continue to be published and excerpted today.

JOHN MUIR

Born in Dunbar, Scotland, on April 20, 1835, Muir immigrated with his family to a homestead near Portage, Wisconsin, in 1849. There, under the harsh hand of a zealot preacher-farmer father, Muir began his quest for understanding wild nature's meaning. From 1859 to 1863 he studied at the University of Wisconsin, taking no degree because of his refusal to follow a curriculum of required courses. He made journeys on foot through the Midwest and Canada and began his study of nature after an accident in 1869 that damaged an eye. That journey is recounted as *A Thousand-Mile Walk to the Gulf.*

Traveling on foot through the untamed West, unarmed and alone for weeks, Muir kept journals that later established his fame as a writer. Articles in the *Overland Monthly* and *Century Magazine* in the 1880s and '90s gave him a national reputation. His first book appeared when he was fifty-six, and only two were published by the time he was seventy.

Multifaceted in his appreciation for the "wildness of nature," Muir's center of interest was the Yosemite Valley. His brilliant articles, which included establishing the valley as the result of glacial action, contributed to the passage of the Yosemite National Park legislation in 1890.

Commemorating Muir's life, writings, and environmental protection efforts, the Muir-Strentzel house stands on a rise surrounded by park-like plantings. Stately Washington palms, the only species of palm native to California, flank the house entrance. The house, constructed and furnished at a cost of $20,000 in 1882, is a rich expression of the Victorian Italianate style with corner quoins, bracketed eaves, and a cupola-topped hip roof; balconies and bay windows offer garden and orchard views. Representing upper-middle-class Victorian life, the house was built almost entirely of redwood, with the exception of Douglas fir floors painted to resemble the period's fashionable light oak.

The generous rooms, with twelve-foot-high ceilings, are furnished in period antiques and a few original family pieces, including an oil painting of Muir by his sister. Heated by seven fireplaces and not electrified until 1914, the east parlor contains one of the few Muir modifications to the original house. Following the great earthquake of 1906 that destroyed several chimneys and damaged the east parlor fireplace, Muir replaced the original marble fireplace with a massive brick Mission-style one where he could build a "real campfire." He also decided to enlarge the parlor by removing a bathroom, once entered by a door that now goes nowhere.

The second floor contains family bedrooms and Muir's study. The hallway was lined with bookshelves full of volumes from his extensive library. In Muir's bedroom, without window curtains, the conservationist could maintain his love of the outdoors and be awakened by the sun.

Muir wrote many of his books and articles on conservation at the original oak desk in the second-floor study. From here he led the cause to establish Yosemite National Park (1890), authored articles to protect endangered forest preserves, and influenced President Theodore Roosevelt to greatly increase the amount of protected public land. He called it his "scribble den," and the desk was characteristically strewn with papers and the floor was littered with manuscript pages. It is reported that Muir would finish a book or article, roll it up, and insert it in the orange crate near his desk. From there, his wife or his daughter Helen would then edit and type the manuscript. The metal cup on the desk was a badge of membership in the Sierra Club. To the left of the desk is a collection of Muir memorabilia, including the yellow hood of his honorary doctorate from Yale University.

The Orchard Trail passes the carriage house and windmill, winding away from the house in the direction of the Martinez Adobe. Built in 1849 the house passed through several owners before being acquired by Dr. Strentzel in 1874, who used it as a storeroom and foreman residence. The two-story house later served as the residence for Muir's eldest daughter, Wanda, and her husband, Thomas Hanna. Three of Wanda's six children were born in the house.

Lassen Volcanic National Park

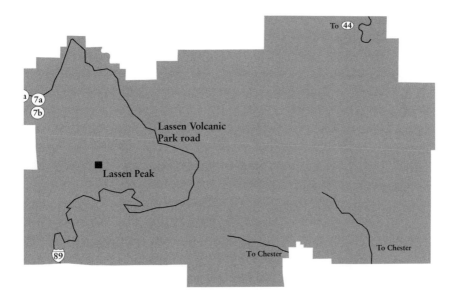

To (44)

a (7a)
(7b)

Lassen Volcanic
Park road

■
Lassen Peak

(89)

To Chester

To Chester

7 Lassen Volcanic National Park (above); Manzanita Lake Entrance Station (facing)

7 Lassen Volcanic National Park
Shasta County, California
www.nps.gov/lavo

Lassen Volcanic National Park is in the northern part of California at the southern end of the Cascade Range, fifty miles west of Interstate 5, connected by California Highways 44 (forty-eight miles east of Redding) and 36 (fifty-two miles east of Red Bluff to the thirty-mile-long Lassen Volcanic Park road (the road that connects State Route 89 through the park, closed in the winter).

■ "On the whole it is difficult to imagine a region where the more striking phenomena of nature are developed on a grander scale."
Professor Douglas W. Johnson

On a still, warm day, Lassen Peak's snow-capped crown casts perfect reflections on Manzanita Lake, a far different scene from that of June 14, 1914, when two weeks of small eruptions climaxed in a massive blast of smoke, ashes, and flying rocks, beginning a seven-year cycle of sporadic volcanic outbursts. In May 1915 a seven-mile-high mushroom cloud and blast of hot gas and lava fragments leveled three square miles of forest and drew the American public's attention. Assumed to be extinct, the peak's eruptions brought national attention and encouraged establishment of the area as Lassen Volcanic National Park in 1916. Until the 1980 eruption of Mount Saint Helens, 10,457-foot-high Lassen Peak, one of the world's largest plug dome volcanoes, was the only volcano in the forty-eight contiguous United States to erupt in the twentieth century.

Mountains created by volcanic activity—including lava flows and volcanic peaks, craters, steam vents and sulfurous boiling springs, and a volcanic plateau dotted with cinder cones and forests—cover the park's 106,000 acres. Designation of Lassen Peak and Cinder Cone as national monuments in 1907 provided protection from encroaching threats of lumbering in the magnificent forests of the Lassen Mountain area. Lassen Volcanic National Park was established August 9, 1916, and incorporated the national monuments.

A day's drive through the western part of the park, starting at the Southwest Entrance, will take you past many of the major landscape features—Sulphur Works, Bumpass Hell, Lassen Peak, Emigrant Pass, Chaos Crags, and Manzanita Lake—and architectural features. The eastern part of the park—a plateau of cinder cones, glacier-carved Warner Valley, boiling hot springs, forests, and rustic buildings—is accessible by some of the park's 150 miles of hiking trails and dead-end unpaved roads.

PETER LASSEN

Peter Lassen, a Danish-born blacksmith, was lured to California by immigrant fever just before the gold rush. He was given a land grant by the Mexican government and established a ranch there with plans to build a town. Needing settlers to populate a town, he set himself up to guide parties to California by way of his "Lassen's Cutoff."

Unfortunately, Lassen was something less than a woodsman, and his circuitous route was extraordinarily difficult, made even harder by his sometimes mistaking what is now the Lassen Peak for Mount Shasta (both are snow-covered mountains). Some of his immigrant parties almost starved and others were outraged when they realized Lassen was often lost. Local legend says that one party forced him at gunpoint to climb the peak that now bears his name to get his bearings. He was usually forgiven when the parties finally reached the comfort and hospitality of his ranch.

7a National Park Service Buildings

The number and quality of historic structures in Lassen Volcanic National Park are modest in comparison to other "crown jewel" national parks. In the early 1930s the National Park Service designed and constructed rustic-style buildings and sites throughout the park: an entrance administrative complex at Manzanita Lake and a fire lookout tower were built of shake-shingled roofs and massive boulders on the lower walls; camp-fire circles at Manzanita Lake campgrounds and Summit Lake were formed by full-round logs, cut out to provide both seats and backs, and half round logs; and log residences for rangers scattered throughout the park.

Park Headquarters is located outside the park, eight miles south in Mineral. The two-story wood-frame building, constructed in 1931, is on a stone-faced concrete foundation with horizontal siding and a steeply pitched shingled roof. Some rustic details are evident in projecting log purlins and brackets under the porch roof, an extension of the main roof.

National Park Service rustic-style buildings at Manzanita Lake, some with alterations in original design and construction, resemble the rustic structures at Crater Lake National Park but without the refinements in scale of boulder walls and finish of workmanship. Consistent in theme, these Manzanita Lake buildings have lower walls of cut stone, reducing in size from foundation to eaves, framing deeply recessed window openings, round-log or timber-roof framing, and shake-shingled roofs. All roofs are uniformly steeply peaked at forty-five degrees.

The earliest of the Manzanita Lake complex buildings, a nine-by-twelve-foot park Entrance Station (1930), retains the original bark-exposed vertical logs at gable ends and decorative wrought-iron lamps on timber brackets. The Ranger Residence (1931) is a one-story structure with massive uncoursed-fieldstone masonry from foundation to eaves, deeply recessed windows, and a recessed corner entrance. An attached garage was added in 1936. The Comfort Station (1931) is a single-story structure, symmetrical in plan and elevations, with massive boulder walls and deep window recesses.

The last building constructed in the administrative complex is the two-story Naturalist's Residence, built in 1933. Construction techniques were similar to the unique approach also used at Crater Lake National Park to fit the short building season. First-floor masonry walls were laid and wooden

7a Manzanita Lake Ranger Residence (above); Entrance Station (below)

formwork was erected with blocked window openings, then concrete was placed between the masonry and formwork. Upper walls are wood-frame construction and gable ends are covered with board-and-batten siding. There is a dormer above the main entrance.

The Horseshoe Lake Ranger Station, built in 1934, is representative of the original rustic Lassen ranger stations. Typical rustic details are log walls of corner notch framing, with sapling-log chinking, sapling window and door surrounds, exposed log-end roof purlins and rafters, and split-shake shingles. A covered porch of peeled log columns and purlins is an extension of the main roof.

The Mount Harkness Fire Lookout, built in 1931, is an example of structures constructed by the National Park Service in parks throughout the Pacific Northwest. Located in the southwest corner of the park, the two-story tower has a stone-masonry first floor and a wood-frame second floor. A log-frame observation platform and windows on all sides of the eighteen-foot-square plan provide sweeping views from the summit of the 8,048-foot-high peak.

7b Mae Loomis Memorial Museum

Unique among Lassen Park buildings are the Loomis Museum and Seismograph Station at Manzanita Lake. Benjamin F. Loomis documented the 1914–15 eruptions and promoted the park's establishment and development. In 1926 he purchased forty acres of privately owned land on Reflection Lake, and in 1927 he and his wife built the Mae Loomis Memorial Museum in memory of their daughter.

Both buildings have reinforced-concrete structural frames and walls clad in gray native volcanic rock of cut-face random-ashlar masonry and topped by crenellated parapets stepped higher at the museum's center front and corners. Short projecting shed overhangs and brackets of concrete clad with Mission-tile roofing cover the museum's entrance, side walls, and all four sides of the seismograph station.

The museum, with walls fifteen feet high, is T-shaped in design. The rectangular main hall is twenty-five by sixty feet. There are ten-by-twelve-foot projections at the rear of the main section. The wide main entrance doors, flanked by sidelight panels and with a Palladian window above, are

7b Mae Loomis Memorial Museum

7b Seismograph Station Building

set in an arched opening. A broad terrace edged by low volcanic-rock masonry walls surrounds the front and both sides of the building. Six square stones in an arched alignment over the entrance are carved with letters for "Museum." Renovated and reopened in 1994, the museum contains a main hall for display and an auditorium.

The smaller Seismograph Station building, measuring approximately ten by twelve feet, is a single-story structure designed to contain seismographic instrumentation. An arched band of stone above the entrance door contains the word "Seismograph."

**8 Manzanar National Historic Site,
dust storm at the War Relocation Authority, 1942**

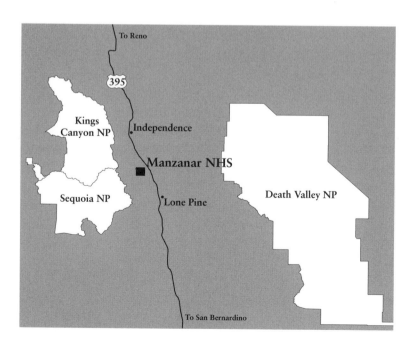

To Reno

395

Kings
Canyon NP

Independence

Manzanar NHS

Sequoia NP

Lone Pine

Death Valley NP

To San Bernardino

8 Manzanar National Historic Site
Independence, Inyo County, California
www.nps.gov/manz

Manzanar is located on the west side of California Highway 395, 220 miles north of Los Angeles and 250 miles south of Reno, Nevada; five miles south of Independence, California; and twelve miles north of Lone Pine, California.

■ "May it serve as a constant reminder of our past so that Americans in the future will never again be denied their constitutional rights and may the remembrance of that experience serve to advance the evolution of the human spirit."

From a plaque at the Relocation Center in Poston, Arizona

The 812-acre Manzanar National Historic Site, established on March 3, 1992, commemorates the World War II internment of Japanese Americans in the Manzanar Relocation Center. Located at the foot of the scenic Sierra Nevada range in the Owens Valley of eastern California, Manzanar has been identified as the most typical of these camps.

From 1942 to 1945 ten thousand Japanese Americans and Japanese legal-resident aliens were interned by the U.S. government on the site of a former agricultural village in the Owens Valley desert. The first of ten detention centers built after President Franklin D. Roosevelt's executive order of February 19, 1942, Manzanar received its first eighty-two residents in March 1942, having been accused of no crime nor given any trial or hearing. Detainees came from Los Angeles; Stockton, California; and Bainbridge Island, Washington. By July the population reached ten thousand. On November 21, 1945, Manzanar was closed; by late 1946 many of the buildings were dismantled and removed from the site. Manzanar was designated a National Historic Landmark in 1985 and authorized as a National Historic Site in 1992.

The center has a tantalizingly scenic view of the eastern face of the Sierra Nevadas from the Owens Valley. However, the mountain range creates a "rain shadow" for the center in a sandy, extremely arid, wind-blown desert region. Blowing dust was everywhere. The weather was utterly miserable—torrid summer heat and bitter winter cold. Through its strength and resourcefulness, the camp population built a community, beautified by gardens and ponds, to overcome the trauma of evacuation and an uncertain future.

PERSONAL JUSTICE DENIED

In 1980 Congress set up a Commission on Wartime Relocation and Internment of Civilians to review the circumstances that led to issuance of the executive order in 1942, to examine the order's impact upon U.S. citizens and permanent resident aliens, and to make recommendations. The commission's report *Personal Justice Denied* stated that "the personal injustice of excluding, removing, and detaining loyal American citizens is manifest. Such events are extraordinary and unique in American history."

In 1988 President Ronald Reagan signed legislation that offered an apology and provided for a payment of $20,000 to each individual interned at centers such as Manzanar.

Laid out on a grid of paved or oiled roads, the 540-acre central area included thirty-six residential blocks containing 576 hastily constructed one-story, 20-by-100-foot wood-frame-and-tarpaper barracks. Partitioned into four or five rooms, an allocation of either a twenty-by-twenty or twenty-by-twenty-four-foot room was made for an entire family. Other residential block buildings included a mess hall, a recreation hall, two communal bathhouses, a laundry room, an ironing room, showers, latrines, and an oil storage tank. Additional blocks in the central area contained an administrative and military police compound, warehouse, garage, and hospital blocks.

All of the buildings were constructed of wood frame, board, and tarpaper. Foundations for the barracks, mess halls, and community buildings were concrete footing blocks set at ten-foot intervals (post and pier). Foundations of the bathhouses, laundry rooms, and ironing rooms were concrete slabs. Although the barracks buildings and block layouts were standardized, the detainees personalized their surroundings by adding sidewalks, entries, rock-lined pathways, gardens, and small ponds. Within firebreaks and the cleared area between the detainee housing and perimeter fence, there were victory gardens and fruit trees restored from neglect after the town of Manzanar was abandoned. A five-strand barbed-wire fence and eight guard towers surrounded the area. Large-scale farming and a chicken farm were located outside the perimeter security fence.

Today the site contains three historic structures: a police post, a sentry post, and the auditorium/gymnasium. There is a one- to two-hour walking tour of the central developed area and a three-mile self-guided auto tour, both of which allow the visitor to grasp the detainees' desolation and distress. More poignant than standing structures are the visible remnants of road grid, foundation slabs, concrete sidewalks and stoops, paved parking areas and gravel walkways, granite and boulder walls, barbed-wire fence posts, broken glass, and the camp cemetery. The barracks area is traced by rows of footing blocks in the brush, sand, and alluvial wash. Remains of the detainee-built gardens, recreation parks, sports facilities, and victory gardens are evidence of valiant efforts to personalize the center, with names, initials, and dates inscribed in concrete, stone-lined walks, and garden complexes.

Two paved roads run east-west from U.S. Highway 395 into the relocation area. Between these two roads are two detainee-constructed buildings, a sentry post and a police post, and a low rock-encircled earthen mound with wooden posts remaining from the relocation center entrance sign. The sentry post (ten by fourteen feet) and the police post (thirteen by fourteen feet) are one-room concrete structures faced with stone. Both buildings have distinctive pagoda-style shake roofs and simulated wood concrete lintels over the doors and windows. Southwest of the entrance, near the site of the administration building, is a thirty-foot-diameter rock-and-concrete planter within a traffic circle. It has many inscriptions listing Japanese American names, hometowns, and dates.

The auditorium, built by the detainees, is a 12,500-square-foot wood-frame building with a low-pitched gambrel roof. The building consists of a central 82-by-125-foot auditorium with a two-story west-side extension for entry and projection booth and a one-story wing along the north side for dressing and rest rooms. A similar wing on the south side of the building was removed in the 1950s, but is planned to be reconstructed. Modifications for use as a vehicle maintenance facility by the Inyo County Road Department altered the original exteriors and interiors.

Original sections of the perimeter fence along State Highway 395 are marked by four-by-four-inch or four-by-six-inch wooden posts approximately sixteen feet apart. They are obviously different from typical range posts because of their height (extending over five feet) and the patterns of nail holes holding wire strands at about twelve-inch intervals, starting at about twelve inches above the ground.

The relocation cemetery is located on the west side of the central fenced portion of the center. At the cemetery there is a large concrete obelisk with Japanese inscriptions on two sides. The inscription on the front (east) side translates as, "Monument to console the souls of the dead." The inscription on the back (west) side translates as, "Erected by the Manzanar Japanese August 1943." Within the fenced cemetery area there are fourteen rock-outlined plots. Across the dirt road, north of the fenced cemetery enclosure, there are three rock-outlined pet graves.

Restoration of the center began with the rebuilding of the perimeter barbed-wire fence enclosing the camp living area. Conversion of the auditorium will provide visitor center/park headquarters. Other planned projects include reconstruction of one of the eight guard towers, a barracks building, and detainee-built garden and ponds.

Visitors to Manzanar National Historic Site are reminded not to disturb the existing remains; removal or disturbance of artifacts is illegal.

Point Reyes National Seashore

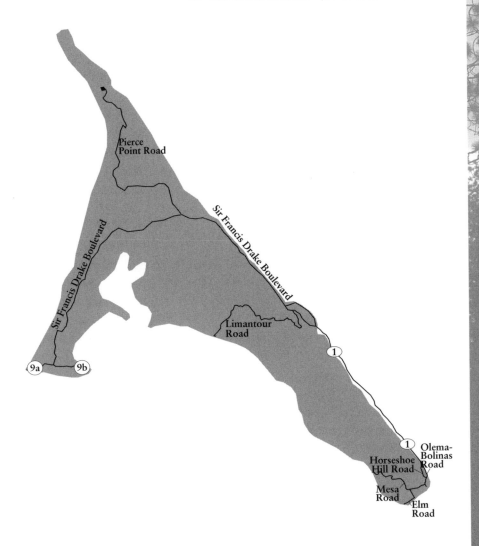

Pierce Point Road

Sir Francis Drake Boulevard

Sir Francis Drake Boulevard

Limantour Road

1

9a 9b

1 Olema-Bolinas Road

Horseshoe Hill Road

Mesa Road

Elm Road

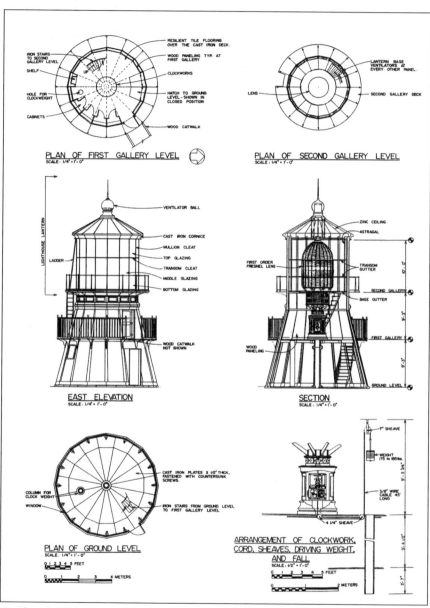

PLAN OF FIRST GALLERY LEVEL
SCALE: 1/4" = 1'-0"

IRON STAIRS TO SECOND GALLERY LEVEL
SHELF
HOLE FOR CLOCKWEIGHT
CABINETS

RESILIENT TILE FLOORING OVER THE CAST IRON DECK.
WOOD PANELING TYP. AT FIRST GALLERY
CLOCKWORKS
HATCH TO GROUND LEVEL - SHOWN IN CLOSED POSITION
WOOD CATWALK

PLAN OF SECOND GALLERY LEVEL
SCALE: 1/4" = 1'-0"

LANTERN BASE VENTILATORS AT EVERY OTHER PANEL.
LENS
SECOND GALLERY DECK

EAST ELEVATION
SCALE: 1/4" = 1'-0"

LIGHTHOUSE LANTERN
LADDER

VENTILATOR BALL
CAST IRON CORNICE
MULLION CLEAT
TOP GLAZING
TRANSOM CLEAT
MIDDLE GLAZING
BOTTOM GLAZING
WOOD CATWALK NOT SHOWN

SECTION
SCALE: 1/4" = 1'-0"

ZINC CEILING
ASTRAGAL
FIRST ORDER FRESNEL LENS
TRANSOM GUTTER
SECOND GALLERY
BASE GUTTER
FIRST GALLERY
WOOD PANELING
GROUND LEVEL

PLAN OF GROUND LEVEL
SCALE: 1/4" = 1'-0"

COLUMN FOR CLOCK WEIGHT
WINDOW

CAST IRON PLATES 2 1/2" THICK, FASTENED WITH COUNTERSUNK SCREWS.
IRON STAIRS FROM GROUND LEVEL TO FIRST GALLERY LEVEL

0 1 2 3 4 5 FEET
0 1 2 3 4 METERS

ARRANGEMENT OF CLOCKWORK, CORD, SHEAVES, DRIVING WEIGHT, AND FALL
SCALE: 1/2" = 1'-0"

7" SHEAVE
WEIGHT 175 to 185 lbs.
3/8" WIRE CABLE 45' LONG
4 1/4" SHEAVE

0 1 2 3 4 5 FEET
0 1 2 METERS

9a Plans for Point Reyes Lighthouse (above); detail (facing)

9 Point Reyes National Seashore
Marin County, California
www.nps.gov/pore

The scenic and winding California Highway 101 provides direct access to the park from the north and south. U.S. 101 farther east is a freeway. East-west roads connect these highways.

North of San Francisco on California Route 1, the 71,000-acre Point Reyes National Seashore is a dramatic landscape of forested ridges, tall cliffs, long beaches, lagoons and estuaries, and offshore bird and sea lion colonies. Separated from northern California by the San Andreas Fault, the Point Reyes Peninsula contains more than 140 miles of hiking trails, campgrounds, three visitor centers, the renovated Pierce Ranch (originally built in 1858), and Point Reyes Lifeboat Station. The park was established on September 13, 1962, and designated a biosphere reserve in 1988.

The Bear Valley Visitor Center and park headquarters near Olema is a barn-shaped structure providing an orientation to the park's roads, trails, and general history. Ken Patrick Visitor Center located at Drake's Beach features exhibits on the peninsula's sixteenth-century maritime history, a 250-gallon saltwater aquarium, a sixteen-foot Minke whale skeleton, and whale fossils. The Point Reyes Lighthouse Visitor Center includes an exhibit center and the Point Reyes Lighthouse.

The seashore was originally the home of the Coast Miwok tribe when Sir Francis Drake arrived in the *Golden Hind* in 1579. After staying five weeks for repairs, Drake sailed west to cross the Pacific on his around-the-world voyage. Explorers from the west came and went, including Cermino in 1595 and Vizcaino in 1603. Settlers arrived nearly two hundred years later; the peninsula's land passed into Mexican hands through land grants and was eventually broken up into dairy ranches until it was established as a national seashore in 1962.

9a Point Reyes Lighthouse

The Point Reyes Lighthouse complex—lighthouse, keeper's quarters, and outbuildings—is one-quarter of a mile and three hundred steps below the visitor center. Built in 1870, the beacon revealed the often fog-shrouded peninsula and warned sailors of the treacherous offshore currents at Point Reyes.

A standard design of the U.S. Lighthouse Board, the freestanding cast-iron light tower of approximately forty feet in height from base to tip of finial is set on two-and-a-half-inch-thick cast-iron plates fixed to the rock of the Point's projection into the ocean. Height from ground to first-gallery level, and first-gallery to second-gallery level, is nine feet three inches; the second gallery is ten feet high to the roof cornice. Wood paneling encloses the ground level up to the second-gallery levels. Walkways circle the tower in the first and second galleries. A cast-iron plate roof caps the light tower.

Exterior access is through a door at the ground level and by the wooden catwalk spanning to an entrance from the first-gallery-level walkway. Internal access from ground level to the first-gallery level—the location of the clockwork mechanism for rotating the lantern—and to the second lantern-gallery level is by internal iron spiral stairs. The restored clockwork on the first-gallery level is visible for inspection. The second gallery cast-iron lantern, still in operation, is a premade ready-to-assemble design that houses a first-order Fresnel lens, which is the largest size placed in service.

9b Point Reyes Lifeboat Station

9b Point Reyes Lifeboat Station

Built in 1927 by the U.S. Life-Saving Service to replace an 1890 station, the Point Reyes Lifeboat Station provided a rescue service at the treacherous peninsula. The station includes a two-story framed boathouse, launchway, officer-in-charge's quarters, and support structures. A typical example of a rail-launching station, with launchway and cradle-launched thirty-six-foot motor lifeboats, the Point Reyes Lifeboat Station is the only unaltered station of this nationally employed type remaining on the Pacific Coast. In its twenty-five years of operation at Point Reyes, the service has saved many lives and lost four of its own.

10a Maritime Museum Building (above) and stairway (facing)

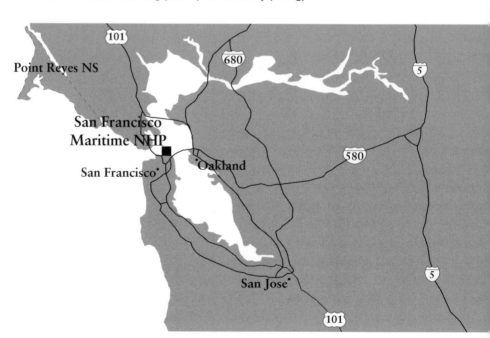

10 San Francisco Maritime National Historic Park

San Francisco, San Francisco County, California
www.nps.gov/safo

The park is at the west end of Fisherman's Wharf, at the Hyde Street cable-car terminus.

The San Francisco Maritime National Historic Park contains a superb example of Streamline Moderne–style architecture, the largest collection of historic sailing ships in the United States, and a Works Progress Administration (WPA) recreational development. Located at the western edge of Fisherman's Wharf and across the street from Ghirardelli Square, the fifty-acre park, established on October 27, 1988, interprets San Francisco's seafaring history. The park consists of two areas open to the public: the Aquatic Park recreational complex (including the Maritime Museum) and a research center (J. Porter Shaw Library) located in the Fort Mason Center. The museum displays models, huge ships' parts, figureheads, and fine arts, and includes the steamship room, which presents the history of West Coast steamers. The Maritime Library houses books, periodicals, and oral histories, and provides access to more than 250,000 photographs, 120,000 pages of ships' plans, and other historic documents. The park boundary also encompasses the Hyde Street Pier, site of the historic vessels display.

10a Aquatic Park Historic District

■ "Ferro-concrete, glass and stainless steel. Its curved ends enclose two per-
fectly circular rooms, the form of which influenced my ideas as how it
might be adequately decorated. . . . The streamlined two hundred and
fifty feet of its length is visible above the eight hundred-foot bathhouse
which is partially underground."

Hilaire Hiler, from *An Approach to Mural Design*

San Francisco's Aquatic Park Historic District is a recreational complex near San Francisco Bay on the site of Black Point Cove. The
masterful design, proposed as early as 1866 by Frederick Law Olmsted and
included in Daniel Burnham's 1905 plan for a major redevelopment of San
Francisco, was developed between 1936 and 1939 as California's most expensive and ambitious Works Progress Administration project.

The group of structures and graceful curve of the municipal pier and
beach facing the ships of the Maritime National Historical Park is an expression of the Streamline Moderne style. Emulating the clean-lined design of
ocean liners, the park has no parallel on the West Coast and, although on a
smaller scale, rivals the design quality of Miami Beach's Art Deco and
Moderne buildings. With minor exceptions, the beach, bathhouse, municipal
pier, rest rooms, concession stand, stadia, and two speaker towers are essentially unchanged from their appearance when completed in 1939. Before
becoming the Maritime Museum and a senior center, the bathhouse served as
a casino and barracks for an antiaircraft corps during World War II.

The bathhouse, now the Maritime Museum building, is a four-story
reinforced-concrete structure designed by the William Moosers, Sr. and Jr.
The building is banked into the slope of land as it gradually descends toward
the bay. The main entrance is on the second floor at the foot of Polk Street.
An oval plan, recessed upper stories, porthole windows, tubular steel railings,
air vents shaped like ship's funnels, and historic white color add to the building's nautical character.

The WPA hired artists Hilaire Hiler, Sargent Johnson, Richard Ayer,
and John Glut to work with the architect designing and decorating the interior. Hiler painted the nautical-motif murals in the main lounge and a study
of the psychological relationship of light and color in the ladies' lounge on
the west end of the second floor. Ayer decorated the third floor, and Johnson

carved the green-slate surround at the entrance portico and supervised the laying of the mosaic tile on the outside balcony of the second floor. John Glut designed the chrome-and-glass light fixtures, and San Francisco sculptor Benjamin Bufano contributed two sculptures—a red seal and a black frog— also on the second-floor balcony.

Inside this ship-shaped, Streamline Moderne structure, mast sections, jutting spars, and figureheads are arranged among the colorful fish and gleaming tiles of muralist Hilaire Hiler's expressionist vision of Atlantis. Displays include panels, videos, oral history re-creations, models, and interactive exhibits. The steamship room illustrates the technological evolution of wind-to-steam power. The *Mermaid*, the one-man sailboat that transported a solo adventurer across the Pacific from Japan in ninety-four days, is displayed on the balcony, along with a statue by Bufano. Second-floor displays include three photomurals of the early San Francisco waterfront, lithographic stones, scrimshaw, and whaling guns.

The concrete stadia flanking the bathhouse, designed for spectators of athletic events and crowds in the lagoon, are now settings for outdoor concerts and a resting place for tourists. The concession stand and the men's rest room are west of the bathhouse at the approach to the Municipal Pier. Designed as part of the Aquatic Park complex, the building reflects the Streamline Moderne character of the bathhouse. The crescent-shaped seawall was built between 1934 and 1938 using granite paving blocks from San Francisco streets.

10b Sailing Ships

The historic ships of Maritime National Historical Park are an eclectic mixture of romantic sailing vessels, military ships, and workhorses of Bay Area commerce. They include the scow schooner *Alma*, square-rigged ship *Balclutha*, schooner *C. A. Thayer*, the river tug *Eppleton Hall*, the ferry *Eureka*, and the ocean tug *Hercules*. All vessels except the *Eppleton Hall* are National Historic Landmarks. Several were spared the scrap yard when acquired by the National Park Service and incorporated into this unusual division of the National Park System. Occasional dry-docking and restoration makes some of the vessels inaccessible at times.

10b Sailing Ship: *Balclutha*

ALMA

Between 1850 and the early 1900s, the best highways around the Bay Area were the waterways, served by flat-bottomed scow schooners like the *Alma*. More than four hundred of these craft were constructed around the San Francisco Bay. Although similar vessels were found in New England and on the shores of the Great Lakes, the basic "scow" design was adapted to local conditions, resulting in a craft uniquely suited to the Bay. Able to navigate the Sacramento/San Joaquin Delta region's shallow creeks, sloughs, and channels, the scows' strong, sturdy hulls could rest safely and securely on the bottom, providing a flat, stable platform for loading and unloading. Their squared bows and sterns not only maximized cargo space but also made scows cheap and easy to build. Typically constructed of inexpensive Douglas fir, their design was so simple that most scows were built "by eye," without plans of any kind.

Built in 1891 by local shipwright Fred Siemer and named after his granddaughter Alma, this flat-bottomed, shallow-draft, sturdy workhorse delivered bulk cargoes from sailing ships to the port. *Alma*'s construction was not unique but it was unusual: her bottom planking was laid athwartship (side to side) instead of fore and aft. Called "log built" because the horizontally laid planks were quite thick, scows like *Alma* traded a bit of speed and ease of repair for economy and strength. Operated as an oyster dredge until 1957, the state of California purchased *Alma* as she lay on the Alviso mudflats in 1959, and restoration work began in 1964. She was transferred to the National Park Service in 1978 and designated a National Historic Landmark in 1988.

BALCLUTHA

The *Balclutha* is a fine example of the square-rigged Cape Horn sailing ship that participated in the grain trade between California and Europe. With a length of 301 feet and the mainmast soaring to 145 feet, she resembles the vessels seen abandoned at San Francisco piers by the gold-rush sailors.

The three-masted full-rigged ship has a hull of steel plates riveted to frames in the "in-and-out system." Since it was built in a time of transition from iron to steel, its deck components are iron. Each mast is a single hollow steel spar instead of lower and topmasts, and above that is a wooden topgallant mast, which also accommodates the royal. She is rigged with single topgallants and royals above double topsails on all three masts and has wire standing rigging set up to turnbuckles. The main deck extends continuously from bow to stern.

Built in Glasgow, Scotland, in 1886, she sailed her maiden voyage to San Francisco. The 140-day trip brought 2,650 tons of coal from Cardiff, Wales, and carried sacks of California grain back to Europe. In 1899 *Balclutha* sailed the Pacific under the Kingdom of Hawaii flag, carrying lumber from the Pacific Northwest to Australia. In 1904 she ran aground and was acquired by the Alaska Packers Association, repaired, and renamed as the salmon packet *Star of Alaska* until retirement in 1930. After a brief life as a movie extra, including *Mutiny on the Bounty*, this popular attraction at the park was purchased by the Maritime Museum in 1954, acquired by the National Park Service in 1978, and designated a National Historic Landmark in 1988.

C. A. THAYER

The *C. A. Thayer* is a surviving example of the sailing schooners that carried lumber to San Francisco from Washington, Oregon, and the California Redwood Coast. Built in 1895, appropriately of Douglas fir, she was named for Clarence A. Thayer, a partner in the San Francisco–based E. K. Wood Lumber Company. Between 1895 and 1912 *C. A. Thayer* usually sailed from Wood's mill in Grays Harbor, Washington, to San Francisco. But she also carried lumber as far south as Mexico, and occasionally even ventured offshore to Hawaii and Fiji.

C. A. Thayer is fairly typical of West Coast, three-masted lumber schooners in size (219 feet extreme) and cargo capacity (575,000 board feet). She carried about half of her load below; the remaining lumber was stacked ten feet high on deck and secured with chain. In port her small crew (eight or nine men) served double duty as longshoremen, so unloading 75,000 to

80,000 feet of board was an average day's work.

After sustaining serious damage during a heavy southeasterly gale, C. A. *Thayer*'s lumber-trade days ended in an Oakland shipyard in 1912. From 1912 to 1924 she engaged in the salmon trade between San Francisco and western Alaska and from 1925 to 1930 served in the cod-fishing waters in the Bering Sea. Purchased by the U.S. Army in 1942, she was refitted with masts and returned to cod fishing until her final voyage in 1950 as the last commercial sailing vessel to operate on the West Coast. Purchased by the State of California in 1957, the Maritime Museum performed more repairs and refitting, and opened C. A. *Thayer* to the public in 1963. The vessel was transferred to the National Park Service in 1978 and designated a National Historic Landmark in 1984.

EPPLETON HALL

Eppleton Hall was built in 1914 by Hepple and Company of South Shields, England, for the Lambton and Hetton Collieries, Ltd. The vessel, named after the Lambton family's ancestral home, was designed to tow oceangoing colliers (coal-carrying vessels) to and from the port of Newcastle on the River Tyne. Coal was a booming business, and towing the sailing vessels upriver to load saved days of transit time. The vessel was also used to tow newly built ships out to sea.

Eppleton Hall, a steam side-wheeler 100½ feet long with side-lever engines, is the only remaining intact example of a Tyne paddle tug. A direct descendant of the first craft to go into commercial service as a harbor tug, the vessel was engaged on the Wear and Tyne Rivers of northeastern England from 1914 to 1967. She was sold for scrap in 1967 and, while sitting on a mud bank, fire destroyed her wooden afterdeck and interior. From 1969 to 1979 she served as a private yacht, during which time she was modified for transit via the Panama Canal to San Francisco, passing through the Golden Gate in March of 1970. The vessel was donated to the National Park Service in 1979.

EUREKA

The paddle-wheel ferry *Eureka* is a reminder of the fleet of ferryboats that once served San Francisco. When in service, *Eureka* could complete a bay crossing in twenty-seven minutes. Built in 1890 at Tiburon, California, for the San Francisco and North Pacific Railway as a freight-car ferry, the originally named *Ukiah* was SF&NPR's "tracks across the Bay," ferrying trains from Sausalito to San Francisco. A side-wheel paddle steamboat from passenger deck up, she is nearly identical fore and aft. Her "double-end" design made disembarking quicker and easier.

Eureka's large "walking beam" steam engine remains intact. Oil was burned in boilers to produce the steam, which drove a huge vertical piston. Perched atop the engine, the walking beam changed this up-and-down motion into rotary motion via a connecting rod linked directly to the paddle-wheel shaft. The twin paddle wheels (each twenty-seven feet in diameter) made twenty-four revolutions per minute.

Modified extensively and rechristened *Eureka*, the vessel slid from the Southern Pacific yard as a passenger and automobile ferry in 1923. The 300-foot-long vessel could carry 2,300 passengers and 120 automobiles. In February 1994 *Eureka* exited San Francisco dry dock after a $2.7 million restoration project for planking caulking, replacement of hull plates, and paddle-wheel support beams. In 1999 the *Eureka* returned to dry dock for repairs to above-water portions of the vessel. It was acquired by the National Park Service and designated a National Historic Landmark in 1985.

HERCULES

The red-stacked *Hercules*, regularly steaming San Francisco Bay with a volunteer crew, joined the San Francisco–based Shipowners' and Merchants' Tugboat Company's Red Stack fleet from Camden, New Jersey, in 1908. Originally purchased as an oceangoing tug, *Hercules* proved its mettle on a maiden voyage by towing sister tug *Goliath* through the Strait of Magellan to San Francisco. Both vessels were oil burners; *Goliath* carried fuel, water, and supplies for her sister, and *Hercules* towed barges, sailing ships, and log rafts between Pacific ports, worked on the construction of the Panama Canal, and towed the first caisson for the naval piers at Pearl Harbor. Because prevailing northwest winds generally made travel up the coast by sail both difficult and circuitous, tugs often towed large sailing vessels to points north of San Francisco.

After acquisition by the Western Pacific Railroad, the 151-foot-long vessel no longer served as an oceangoing tug but shuttled railroad car barges back and forth across San Francisco Bay. She worked until 1962, when decline of the railroads and the introduction of diesel-powered tugs sealed her fate. *Hercules* avoided the scrap yard, but languished until the California State Park Foundation acquired her in 1975. The National Park Service took over the task of her restoration in 1977, and in 1986 she was designated a National Historic Landmark.

WAPAMA

In the nineteenth and twentieth century, wooden-hulled schooners served the Pacific Coast lumber trade. Launched in 1915, *Wapama* is the last survivor of a fleet of more than two hundred ships engaged in maritime trade and coastal commerce carrying lumber, general cargo, and passengers. The *Wapama* is on view at the Maritime National Historic Park.

Other historic ships open to the public near the San Francisco Maritime National Historic Park are the Liberty Ship SS *Jeremiah O'Brien* and the submarine *Pampanito*.

JEREMIAH O'BRIEN

Located at Pier 3, Fort Mason Center, the SS *Jeremiah O'Brien* is open to the public as a floating memorial dedicated to those Americans who built, loaded, sailed, or died aboard Liberty Ships during World War II. One of 2,751 maritime cargo carriers designed for wartime service, the *Jeremiah O'Brien* participated in the D-Day invasion, later served in the Pacific, and is the only unaltered surviving World War II Liberty Ship still operative. In the spring of 1994 a group of dedicated volunteers sailed the SS *Jeremiah O'Brien* under her steam from San Francisco to Normandy for the fiftieth anniversary of D-Day. Although built in Portland, Maine, in 1943, the *Jeremiah O'Brien* is typical of the hundreds of Liberty ships built in Bay Area shipyards in World War II. The National Liberty Ship Memorial, founded in 1978 specifically to restore the ship, manages the ship through a cooperative agreement with the National Park Service.

PAMPANITO

Approximately five blocks from the Hyde Street Pier at Pier 45 in Fisherman's Wharf, rocking silently in the San Francisco Bay swell, the submarine *Pampanito* (named for a fish found in Pacific waters) recalls the lethal power of the underwater fleet supporting the island-hopping campaign that led to the World War II victory against Japan. Built at the Portsmouth, New Hampshire, naval shipyard and commissioned November 6, 1943, it made six war patrols, is credited with sinking five Japanese ships, and earned six battle stars. Decommissioned in 1945, the *Pampanito* is managed as a floating museum by the National Maritime Museum Association.

Sequoia and Kings Canyon National Parks

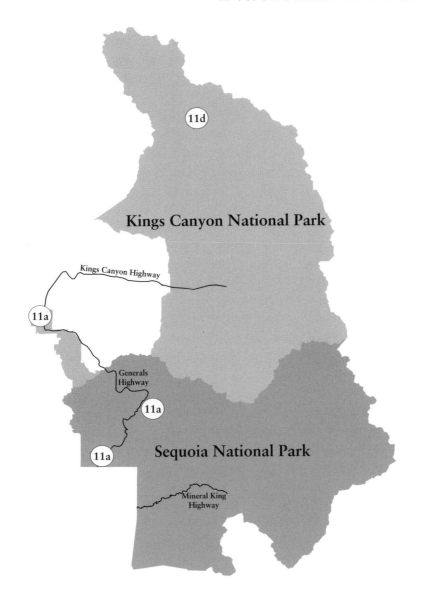

Kings Canyon National Park

Kings Canyon Highway

Generals Highway

Sequoia National Park

Mineral King Highway

11d

11a

11a

11a

11a Ash Mountain Entrance Sign (above); view along Mineral King Highway (facing)

11 Sequoia and Kings Canyon National Parks

Fresno and Tulare Counties, California

www.nps.gov/seki

The parks are due east of Fresno (via California Highway 180) and Visalia (via California Highway 198). Generals Highway connects the roads, making loop trips possible. There is no access to the parks from the east.

■ "The Big tree *(Sequoia gigantea)* is Nature's forest masterpiece, and, as far as I know, the greatest of Living things."
John Muir, *Our National Parks*

Sequoia and Kings Canyon, the twin national parks at the southern end of California's Sierra Nevada, have as diverse ecosystems as any national park in the country. On a clear day, the snowcapped peaks of the Sierra that bound the parks on the east are visible from Fresno, fifty-five miles to the west. In between are arid foothills, forest belts that include stands of giant sequoia, and alpine terrain. This land so entranced John Muir that he set out countless times to roam among the Sierra heights to document the redwood groves ravaged by logging enterprises and the foothill grasslands overgrazed by sheep.

Sequoia National Park was established on September 25, 1890, and General Grant National Park (now Kings Canyon) on October 1, 1890. Only Yellowstone predates Sequoia as a national park. Between 1920 and 1940, campaigns to enlarge the parks succeeded in extending the boundaries to the north and east to include more stands of sequoia and high-peak country. General Grant National Park was incorporated into Kings Canyon National Park in 1940. The last addition to the twin parks was Mineral King in 1978, added to the southern part of Sequoia National Park to avoid its being developed as a ski resort on Forest Service lands. As a wartime economy measure, the parks were placed under single administration in 1943, and the arrangement proved so effective that it has continued to this day. These two national parks, surrounded by national forests and wilderness areas, comprise approximately 1.6 million acres.

For many years the "Big Trees" attracted only a modest number of visitors; in 1909 the superintendent reported 854 tourists at Sequoia and 798 at General Grant. The number had increased to more than 10,000 a year when the National Park Service was created in 1916. Today, Sequoia and Kings Canyon receive approximately two million visitors annually.

Only the western quarter of Sequoia and Kings Canyon is accessible to automobiles. The eastern three-quarters, mostly High Sierra, have been set aside as wilderness. There is no road access from Highway 395 on the east side. Vehicle access is by Highway 180 from Fresno into Sequoia, or by Highway 198 from Visalia into Kings Canyon. Within the parks a convenient loop on the Generals Highway, aptly named after the General Sherman and General Grant trees, is the world's premier giant sequoia thoroughfare. Kings Canyon Highway (Highway 180) begins at Grant Grove and heads east eighty-five miles through the canyons of the Kings River South Fork, ending at Copper Creek. Mineral King Highway is a twenty-five-mile route of switchbacks through sublime scenery, ending at the vista of 10,587-foot-high Farewell Gap.

THE GIANT SEQUOIA

The giant sequoia has a column-like trunk more than thirty feet in diameter, huge stout branches, cinnamon-colored bark, and it grows only on the western slope of the Sierra Nevada between 5,000 and 7,000 feet in elevation. Also called "Sierra Redwood" and "Big Tree," its scientific name is Sequoiadendron giganteum. The Giant Sequoia General Sherman is the world's largest living thing, with a basal diameter of thirty-six feet and a height of 274.9 feet. The Coast Redwood, Sequoia semper-

virens, taller and usually only eight to ten feet in diameter and more conifer-like in appearance, is found in a narrow strip along the Pacific Coast. Its common name comes from the color of its heartwood, not its gray bark. A third species, the Dawn Redwood, is indigenous to China.

The examples of important historic structures at Sequoia and Kings Canyon are the result of the parks' growth and development over a century and a half of settlement, and the stewardship of the National Park Service. In contrast to the excellent examples of rustic architecture found elsewhere in the National Park System, it would seem that the extraordinary scenery of Sequoia and Kings Canyon confirmed the Grosvenors' claim in the pages of *National Geographic:* "In that architecture which is voiced in the glorious temples of the Sequoia grove . . . there is a majesty and an appeal that the mere handiwork of man, splendid though it may be, can never rival."

The earliest historic structures at Sequoia and Kings Canyon National Parks are a scattering of nineteenth-century settlers' cabins built out of felled sequoias. Summer colonies on private inholdings at Wilsonia, Silver City, and Kings Canyon also contain small-scale buildings rustic in character; these wood-frame cabins, often on post-and-block foundations, suggest impermanence. Although National Park Service master plans proposed unifying architectural themes for major visitor areas, only the Giant Forest/Lodgepole and Grant Grove areas nestled among the sequoia groves demonstrate a rustic woodsy character. These rustic structures are modest in scale and were gradually added over the years along simpler architectural themes than those in other national parks.

The influence of railroaders and private entrepreneurs on building development was not felt in these parks, and there are no grand Rustic hotels or extensive tourist complexes. The Southern Pacific Railroad lobbied for national park designation with a goal of preventing lumbering of the sequoia to compete with their own resources. Tent camps satisfied the needs of the early visitors and campers who arrived from the California Central Valley. A day trip provided relief from the heat of the lowlands and satisfied most visitors and self-sufficient hikers. The National Park Service eventually addressed the issue of visitor facilities and initiated concessioner developments at Grant Grove and Giant Forest.

When Stephen Mather became director of the National Park Service (1916), there were only a few service buildings in the parks. They followed the basic principles of rustic design, using features that would be incorporated in later developments. The harsh climate of the high country placed special demands on the framing and exterior materials used at Giant Forest, Grant Grove, Lodgepole, and Cedar Grove. These buildings are principally characterized by small-scale designs that allow them to follow the site's natural contours of exposed redwood frames with infilled walls and low-pitched gable roofs. Several utility buildings were soon erected; simple in mass and form, they were compatible with the setting because of the color and texture of the exterior materials and their size and scale.

The newly created National Park Service Landscape Engineering Division, under the direction of Daniel Hull, began designs for an administrative complex at Giant Forest in 1921. The administration building, superintendent's residence, and employee cabins were all patterned after the earlier utility buildings. At the same time, concession developments built at Giant Forest and Grant Grove included lodges and cabins designed by Gilbert Stanley Underwood and Herbert Maier.

Although no single design dominated the federal work at the two parks, the National Park Service buildings share common rustic features. These are most visible in the Giant Forest Lodge Market designed by Gilbert Stanley Underwood, the ranger residence at Giant Forest (1931) designed by Merel Sager, and the comfort stations and ranger stations scattered throughout the parks built in the 1930s. The designers are credited with understanding that natural stone would play an unimportant, inconspicuous scenic role within the dense forest setting.

At the same time, it was impossible to erect buildings truly proportional to the setting; even the smallest nearby sequoias were often greater than ten feet in diameter. Buildings were framed with ten-inch-square redwood timbers. To give the buildings a proper relationship to the surrounding forest, siding—sometimes of unplaned lap; resawn, or tongue-and-groove planking; or shakes—provided an infill between the timber posts. Multi-light casement windows and doors were inserted in the bays between the posts. The park service buildings' exterior walls are a dark chocolate brown; the concessions buildings are a medium reddish-brown similar to the color of sequoia bark. Central gable shake-covered roofs, with vertical board-and-batten ends, were often joined by smaller elements to reduce the overall mass. A narrow foundation of rubble granite masonry over concrete from the ground to the floor line provides continuity with the stone chimneys.

Changes in the man-made landscape of Sequoia and Kings Canyon National Parks evolved through natural causes and planned restoration of the fragile sequoia grove environment. Some buildings were relocated, others damaged by fire and heavy snow loads. An extensive National Park Service planning process in the 1990s resulted in the removal of many structures from the Giant Forest area to protect the sequoia groves' fragile environment.

Readily accessible historic architecture is found in close proximity to the parks' major automobile routes. Ranger stations on hiking trails present fine examples of National Park Service rustic architecture. The adventurous hiker can find the Muir Hut on the John Muir Trail at an elevation of 11,955 feet.

11a The Generals Highway

ASH MOUNTAIN

Route 198 leads into the Generals Highway at the Ash Mountain entrance. Less than a quarter-mile inside the park is a massive, sequoia wood sign carved in 1936 by a Civilian Conservation Corps enrollee from Arkansas. The rustic character of the stepped granite foundation, wrought-iron supporting bracket, simple block lettering, and overall hand-crafted nature of the roughly worked wood initiates the visitor at the entrance to a special place separate from the outside world.

Beyond the entrance sign is the park headquarters with administrative offices, staff quarters, and visitor center. Although a 1930s master plan called for predominance of "Spanish-Californian style" buildings—suitable for the park's lower foothill elevations—concern for fireproofing limited the style to the superintendent's residence. The lack of a unifying design style produced a mixture of unappealing construction, seen in the pole frame and shingle-sided buildings as well as the utilitarian modern buildings.

GIANT FOREST

The Generals Highway climbs to more than 6,000 feet in elevation in the sixteen miles from the Ash Mountain entrance to Giant Forest, site of some of the finest groups of giant sequoia. Once the location of the rustic Camp Kaweah and Giant Forest Village Lodge and guest cabins, only vestiges remain of the National Park Service in the presence of the Giant Forest

Market, ranger residence, and comfort station. The Giant Forest area was restored to as pristine a state as possible, with the removal of almost 300 shake-exterior cabins, tent cabins, and exterior framing support buildings.

The Giant Forest Market (now the Giant Forest Museum), designed by Gilbert Stanley Underwood and constructed in 1928–29, expressed the National Park Service's intentions for Sequoia National Park. The heavy exposed frame, symmetry in the broken masses of the building's wings, heavy wrought-iron hardware, multi-light transoms and display windows, paired entrance doors with herringbone patterns, and the exterior dark red-brown color and lichen-green window trim—all express a rustic design ethic. The ranger residence (masterfully sited by landscape architect Merel Sager) and comfort station have common features in their granite foundations, exposed structural frames, and cedar-shingle roofs.

Visitors can see early settler shelters from trails in the Giant Forest area. The Squatter's Cabin and Cattle Cabin are preserved examples of frontier log cabins, built of corner-notched peeled logs and gable-end cedar shake roofs. A more unusual preserved shelter is Tharp's Log, combining a downed fire-hollowed giant sequoia with a frame structure complete with granite chimney. Branching off from the Generals Highway at the west end of Giant Forest Village is the Moro Rock/Crescent Meadow. Along this route are the Auto and Tunnel logs. From the Moro Rock parking area, four hundred steps of the Moro Rock Trail, ascend three hundred feet to the summit of Moro Rock. The climb to a 6,735-foot elevation is rewarded with spectacular views of the Sequoia National Park foothills, the San Joaquin Valley, and on clear days, the Coast Range more than one hundred miles to the west.

HALE D. THARP

Hale D. Tharp came to the Placerville gold fields in 1852 but soon moved to Tulare County to enter the cattle business. He arrived in the foothills near the lower Kaweah River in 1856 looking for a cattle range. In 1858 he persuaded two of the Potwisha tribe living in the area around Hospital Rock (near the Ash Mountain park entrance inside the park boundary) to guide him to their meadows and a sight of the fabled red-barked trees. The trip took him past Moro Rock and into what is now known as Giant Forest. Tharp returned in 1860 with his stepsons, climbed Moro Rock, and established a squatter's claim in the vicinity of Crescent

Meadow. In 1869, after he had hewn a trail wide enough to accommodate livestock, Tharp trailed his first herd into Giant Forest. Seeking shelter for herdsmen, Tharp found a huge downed, fire-hollowed sequoia log and ingeniously framed its end with a cabin fitted with a door, window, and chimney.

The Generals Highway passes Lodgepole, a mixture of buildings that includes a visitor center, seasonal staff housing, and the Lodgepole Market Center—an unsuccessful attempt at a modern interpretation of the National Park Service rustic style. Immediately beyond Lodgepole, hand-cut stone-arch bridges at Marble Creek and a half-mile farther at Clover Creek mark the beginning of thick mixed-conifer forests. Similar in design, the Marble Creek Bridge (a 45-foot-arch span built in 1930–31) and Clover Creek Bridge (a 90-foot-arch span built in 1931) illustrate the National Park Service's attention to integrating site structures with the surroundings. Spanning granite gorges, the concrete structures are faced with eighteen- to twenty-four-inch granite masonry walls. The hollow structures formed by the arch and stone walls were filled with dirt and topped with the asphalt roadbed of the Generals Highway.

The Generals Highway continues beyond recent development at Wuksachi Village. At Clover Creek and nearby Dorst Campground is the Cabin Creek Ranger Station and Dormitory. Ten miles beyond Clover Creek, a massive, hand-carved redwood sign marks the boundary of the Sequoia National Park and Sequoia National Forest; ten miles later the road reenters the park. Approaching Grant Grove there is a side trip to Wilsonia, a private community of summer cabins.

GRANT GROVE VILLAGE

Grant Grove Village once was the headquarters of the old General Grant National Park established close to the same time as Sequoia National Park in 1890. The four square miles of land around the General Grant tree were eventually expanded and incorporated into Kings Canyon National Park in 1940. Located in the village are the visitor center, rustic cabins, staff residences, and support buildings.

The predominance of rustic buildings shows the influence of National Park Service plans in the area. The former Superintendent's Residence of General Grant National Park is a classic rustic structure of lap siding,

11a Giant Forest Lodge

alternating shingle patterns in the gable ends, wood-shingle roof, beveled out-lookers at the eaves, and a finely constructed granite chimney. Less elegant but retaining rustic features are the other permanent residences in the area. The village cabins designed by Gilbert Stanley Underwood are more important as a collection of structures and the sense of place they create than the individual buildings. The cabins are simple frame structures, either duplexes or single cottages, with shake siding, wood-shingle roofs with double-coursing every fifth row, six-light casement windows, thick plank doors with wrought-iron hardware, and the traditional dark reddish-brown color with lichen green trim.

The Gamlin Cabin, near the 267-foot-tall General Grant sequoia, evokes a rugged frontier image with visible broadaxe marks on the building's wood. The size of the logs and planks—massive squared corner-notched logs, three tiers of redwood roof planks, hewn boards set vertically in the gable ends—sets a rugged frontier image in scale with the surrounding landscape.

11a Gamlin Cabin

11b Kings Canyon Highway

Leaving Grant Grove, California Highway 180 (Kings Canyon Highway) winds through more than twenty miles of Sequoia National Forest and reenters Kings Canyon National Park. The scenic lower V-shaped canyons of the drive carved by the south fork of the King River change into a glacial carved U-shaped canyon at the entrance to Kings Canyon National Park. Incorporated into the park in 1965, Kings Canyon is an eight-mile-long glacial gorge that extends from Lewis Creek at the park's boundary to Zumwalt Meadows at road's end. John Muir considered the canyon a rival to Yosemite Valley. "It is about ten miles long," Muir wrote, "half a mile wide, and the stupendous rocks of purplish gray granite that form the walls are from 200 to 5,000 feet in height, while the depth of the valley below the general surface of the mountain mass from which it has been carved is considerably more than a mile."

Historic architecture in the canyon is located at Cedar Grove: the

Visitor Center (1930), Naturalist Residence (1935), and Guest Minister Residence (1933), the latter built by the Forest Service as a storage shed. The Visitor Center, constructed by the U.S. Forest Service and Civilian Conservation Corps as a ranger station, is a three-room building of log walls and log corner posts, shake-shingle roof, horizontal shake gable ends, and the brown color characteristic of the National Park Service. Beyond Zumwalt Meadows at road's end are trails leading into mountain canyons with National Park Service and trappers' log cabins: the Roaring River Snow survey cabin; the Lackey cabin at Scaffold Meadow, Roaring River; and the "Shorty" Lovelace cabins. Joseph Walter "Shorty" Lovelace (1886–1963) trapped throughout Kings Canyon for more than twenty years until the park's creation in 1940 and built one-room log cabins at Vidette Meadow (Bubbs Creek), Gardiner Creek, Woods Creek, Cloud Canyon, Granite Pass, and Sphinx Pass.

11c Mineral King Highway

In the 1870s the mining town of Mineral King offered prospects of another Comstock Lode, and a road was built into the Valley. The mines never produced much silver, but the road remains, with a destination of incomparable beauty at its end, although one with few historic architectural structures. Settlers' cabins, U.S. Forest Service subdivisions with private cabins, National Park Service structures, and remains of villages and mills are visible along the sublime journey to the high country.

At a junction of California Highway 198 at Hammond west of the Sequoia National Park boundary, the narrow, steep, and often tortuously winding Mineral King Highway rises in twenty-five miles from an elevation of 1,100 to 7,800 feet at road's end. From two miles east of Hammond to the bridge over the east fork of the Kaweah River (6 ½ miles east of Hammond), trestlework is seen attached to the bluffs above the road. This wooden "ditch" supported on a timber trestle is the Number One Flume of the Whitney Power Company. Beginning in 1898 the Kaweah hydroelectric system was developed over twenty years by the Whitney Power Company. Flumes in the park, completed in 1913, bring water from the Middle and Marble Forks of the Kaweah River to the powerhouse outside the park near Ash Mountain.

The dead-end road continues past the Atwell Mill Ranger's Station and private recreational cabins at Cabin Cove. At twenty miles from Hammond, Silver City is a private community with private cabins, guest cabins, a restaurant, and a small store. The name comes from the silver rush when eager miners camped here waiting for the snows to melt in the valley above. Three miles east of Silver City is Faculty Flat, developed mainly by teachers and professors from the Los Angeles area in the 1930s. Finally, after ninety minutes of arduous driving, the traveler is rewarded with the site of rustic private cabins in the spectacular setting of Mineral Valley.

11d High Country

This is a vast region of unbroken wilderness, of mountains, canyons, rivers, lakes, and meadows. Ranger stations and hikers' huts are found along some of the most spectacular hiking trails in all the national parks in the high country of Sequoia and Kings Canyon National Parks. Ranger stations are located at South Fork, Quinn Creek, Hockett Meadow, Little Five Lakes, Rowell Meadow, Kern Canyon, Rock Creek, Tyndall Creek, Bearpaw Meadow, Pear Lake, Charlotte Lake, Rae Lakes, LeConte Canyon, and McLure Meadow.

The John Muir Hut at Muir Pass on the John Muir Trail is in the northern corner of Kings Canyon National Park. Emerging from granite mountaintop rubble, the intriguing profile of the native granite structure with course ashlar-pattern walls, on an octagonal base about twenty feet in diameter, is stepped to form a vaulted dome twenty feet high. A stone chimney protrudes from a corner of the dome.

12 El Capitan, Yosemite National Park

Yosemite National Park

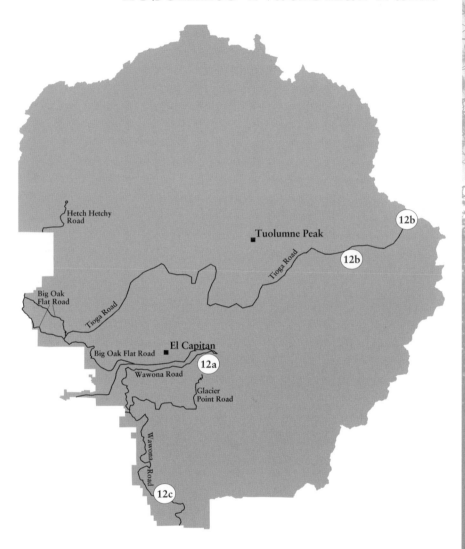

Hetch Hetchy
Road

Tuolumne Peak

12b

12b

Tioga Road

Big Oak
Flat Road

Tioga Road

Big Oak Flat Road

El Capitan

12a

Wawona Road

Glacier
Point Road

Wawona Road

12c

12c Moore Cottage, The Wawona Hotel (above); Tioga Pass Entrance Station, detail (facing)

12 Yosemite National Park
Mariposa County, California
www.nps.gov/yose

There are four entrances to the park: the south entrance on California Highway 41N from Fresno, the Arch Rock entrance on Highway 140W from Merced, the Big Oak Flat entrance on Highway 120W from Modesto and Manteca, and the Tioga Pass entrance on Highway 120E from Lee Vining and U.S. 395.

■ "Nowhere will you see the majestic operations of nature more clearly revealed beside the frailest, most gentle and peaceful things. Nearly all the park is a profound solitude. Yet it is full of charming company, full of God's thoughts, a place of peace and safety amid the most exalted grandeur and eager enthusiastic action, a new song, a place of beginnings abounding in first lessons of life, mountain-building, eternal, invincible, unbreakable order; with sermons in stones, storms, trees, flowers, and animals brimful of humanity."

John Muir, *Our National Parks*

Yosemite National Park's 761,266 acres contain glacial valleys, waterfalls of extraordinary height, giant sequoias, alpine meadows, Sierra peaks, lakes, and streams. This vast place of scenic grandeur has enchanted the imagination of the American public since the 1850s when reports and photographs of it first began to appear. John Muir, ecological visionary and the champion of protecting America's wilderness, described the challenge of portraying Yosemite in *Our National Parks:*

■ "But to get all this into words is a hopeless task. The leanest sketch of each feature would need a whole chapter. Nor would any amount of space, however industriously scribbled, be of much avail. To defraud town toilers, parks in magazine articles are like pictures of bread to the hungry. I can write only hints to incite good wanderers to come to the feast."

And a feast it is: El Capitan, soaring to 3,900 feet above the valley at 7,569 feet; Half Dome's knife-cleaved face at 8,824 feet; Sentinel Dome at 8,122 feet; Yosemite Falls cascading 2,425 feet; and the diaphanous Bridalveil Falls plunging 620 feet. Yosemite's adjective-spilling grandeur is more than just the valley, less than one percent of the national park. Away from the concentrated crowds of valley visitors there is a lifetime of scenic experiences and historic architecture features along the valley's El Portal Road, the east-west Big Oak Flat Road, and Tioga Road from the Big Oak Flat entrance to the Tioga Pass entrance, Glacier Point Road; and the Wawona Road (California Highway 41). Close to the south entrance are Mariposa Grove, Wawona, and the Pioneer Yosemite History Center.

The dramatic valley, with 3,000-foot granite walls, was not entered by non-Europeans until 1851. Within a few years, tourists began to seek it out. Horace Greeley visited the valley in 1859 and pronounced it "the most unique and majestic of nature's marvels." The *Boston Evening Transcript* published eight articles by Thomas Starr King in 1860 and 1861 that aroused a great deal of interest. Soon, hotels were opened, toll roads built, and a stage line started. By 1864 the press of tourism along with concern about overdevelopment and overgrazing threatened the valley's beauty.

President Lincoln signed a congressional bill in 1864 granting the valley and the Mariposa Grove of Big Trees to California "to be held for public use, resort, and recreation, inalienable for all time." Frederick Law Olmsted, who was appointed a commissioner of the state grant, wrote a landmark report in

1865, *The Yosemite Valley and the Mariposa Big Tree Grove*, recommending public use and enjoyment in accordance with the philosophy of the grant. Olmsted's report formulated the philosophic base for the creation of state and national parks. A national park was created around the original grant in 1890, and the state lands were returned to the federal government in 1906.

Yosemite's complex terrain and climate presented a tantalizing challenge to painters, photographers, and writers. Albert Bierstadt's paintings, Carleton Watkins's early photographs, and John Muir's energetic prose inspired the decision to officially preserve the valley and trees. Ansel Adams devoted a lifetime to recording memorable images of the eloquent light, the dramatic forms of massive granite, and the play of the seasons in the valley and the Sierra.

The experience of Yosemite for most travelers is bound to the valley, the place that historically accounts for the very existence of Yosemite as a national park. A deep gorge, seven miles long, one mile wide, and three thousand feet deep, is as breathtaking today as it was when sighted by miners pursuing a wounded bear over a century and a half ago. But beyond the valley, to the north and south, are less-traveled routes of equally dramatic scenery and compelling historic structures. The Tioga Road, to the north, crosses east and west through Tuolumne Meadows and the high country; leading south out of the valley, the Wawona Road passes Discovery View, the historic Wawona Hotel, and carries on to the Mariposa Grove of giant sequoias.

12a Yosemite Valley

A tour of historic architecture in Yosemite Valley follows the one-way pattern of roads.

YOSEMITE VALLEY CHAPEL

This New England–style, 250-seat chapel was built under the sponsorship of the California State Sunday School Association in the summer of 1879. Designed by Charles Geddes, a San Francisco architect, it originally stood near the base of Four-Mile Trail, a mile or so down the valley from the present site. The chapel was remodeled and moved in 1901. The building was acquired by the National Park Service in 1927 and completely restored in 1982.

The chapel is the only building left at the site of the old Yosemite village. Stephen Mather's personal interest in Yosemite Valley led to one of his first actions as director of the National Park Service: the relocation of the old commercial village to a new site on the north side of the Merced River, warmed by the winter sun. Mather accepted a new village plan in 1923. Gradually, the old buildings were removed, some to the new village or to the Pioneer Village at Wawona. All remnants of the old village were finally removed in 1980. There were good reasons for the relocation of the old village, besides its unsightly and disorganized character, as illustrated by a disastrous flood in December 1937. An overnight rain of almost twelve inches put the valley awash, and rescuers had to wade into the chapel to save the organ, pew cushions, and hymnals. Floods frequently threatened the chapel, as recently as 1997. The chapel's foundations were raised after the flood of 1964.

The original structure consisted of a single room twenty-six by fifty feet, with a stone foundation, exterior board-and-batten walls painted dark brown with light trim, a shingle roof, bell tower, and steeple. The original interior included pews, an altar, coal-oil lamp fixtures, vertically planked walls, beaded ceiling planking, and exposed wooden scissor trusses. The organ was donated in the memory of Florence Hutchings, the first child of European descent born in Yosemite. The chapel offices were built in 1953.

CAMP CURRY (CURRY VILLAGE)

Camp Curry, located at the base of Glacier Point at the eastern end of Yosemite Valley, is a village of more than four hundred canvas tent cabins (wood platforms and canvas walls and roof) and wooden cabins (some with baths) massed in closely aligned areas. A collection of permanent buildings at the camp entrance includes offices, a camp store, cafeteria, fast-food restaurants, lodge, and post office. The site is strewn with boulders, and conifers are scattered throughout the guest-cabin area. The convenient location is within walking distance of most of the valley's major attractions.

The camp's architectural value is found primarily in the collective grouping of buildings and the rustic experience provided for guests and visitors. Although the site contains a few structures of architectural significance and some recent additions, Camp Curry exhibits a continuity of scale and texture, characterized by rustic materials of river stone foundations, unpeeled logs and bark strips, horizontal- or diagonal-sawn exteriors, and strongly expressed structural members. The buildings express a low profile through gable or hipped roofs with wide overhanging eaves and a uniform dark color for all buildings but the tents. The tent cabins, packed closely in ranks and rows, recall more than a century of traditional rustic camping at Yosemite.

David and Jennie Curry established their innovative camp in 1899. As an alternative to the Sentinel Hotel and public campgrounds, the Currys believed that a tent camp, offering a minimum of services and thus economical for guests, would be a success. The camp opened with seven tents, expanding to twenty-five tents by summer's end, and, with the help of a student labor force, accommodated 292 guests the first summer. The legendary hospitality of David Curry lasted until his death in 1917. The Yosemite Park and Curry Company carried on the camp's traditions of nightly campfires, low rates, and warm hospitality; the dramatic "firefall" from Glacier Point continued until terminated by the National Park Service in 1969.

Over the years, fires, new construction, and rehabilitation of existing structures have modified early structures, although changes are generally sympathetic to the surrounding environment. Seen in their original condition are the rustic Camp Curry entrance sign (circa 1914), Old Registration Office (1904, now lounge and postal facilities), Foster Curry cabin (1916), Mother Curry's bungalow (1917), bungalows with baths (1918–22), cabins without baths (1930s), and auditorium/dance hall (1913, converted to Stoneman House with guest rooms).

LeConte Memorial Lodge

The unusual granite LeConte Memorial Lodge, with unique Tudor influences, was built in 1903 by the Sierra Club to serve as a library and club information center. Because of the inspiration of their founding president, John Muir, the Sierra Club's dedication to wilderness preservation is rooted in the Yosemite region. Mountaineering expeditions originated at the lodge, and lectures by Muir inspired members to defend the valley and influence conservation matters related to the public domain. When an early member of the club, Joseph LeConte, died at Yosemite in 1901, his friends decided to establish a living memorial in his name.

The original location of the lodge was on a gentle rise of ground against a background of trees and the granite walls of Glacier Point. The owner of nearby Camp Curry needed space for additional guest accommodations and prevailed upon the club to move the lodge a short distance to the west. The roof was dismantled, most of the original stonework was saved, and the lodge was rebuilt according to the original plans. It reopened in the summer of 1919. Beginning in 1920, a young San Franciscan named Ansel Adams worked for the next four years as its summer custodian.

The lodge's style and execution are unique in the National Park System. They derived from the emerging appreciation of the California rustic landscape as expressed by a group of San Francisco Bay Area architects. One of the leaders of this group, Bernard Maybeck, searched for innovative ways to relate a structure to its site through building massing and the use of natural materials. Maybeck greatly influenced the work of his brother-in-law, John White, the architect of LeConte Memorial Lodge. Both believed that a building's site and the choice of construction materials had a strong influence on the building's design. Architectural interest was provided by form and exposed structural framing on the interior; ornamentation or decorative detail was not necessary.

The verticality of the lodge, emphasized by an exaggerated pyramid roof and weathered granite walls, reflects the steep pitches of the granite cliffs surrounding Yosemite Valley. Symmetrically Y-shaped in plan, the building is dominated by the massive wood-shingled roof and gable rough-cut stone end walls. Entrance steps lead to a hexagonal porch defined by the lodge's granite walls and low parapet walls that extend from the gable ends. The roof is the lodge's dominant architectural feature on both the exterior and interior. An unusual hammer-beam structure, it rests on engaged stone piers built into the walls, and supports exposed scissor trusses above the interior spaces. The steep pitches and shapes of the roof and the parapet walls emphasize the verticality of the structure. On the interior, the exposed roof structure and the chimney, which extends from the fireplace to the roof, reinforce this.

RANGERS' CLUB

When Stephen Mather decided to relocate Yosemite Village to the valley's north side, the Rangers' Club and garage were the first major structures built there. Mather saw the need for a special structure to house the newly organized ranger force, and he decided to personally finance the construction. His aim was to entice Congress into building clubhouses in other parks, but the idea never took hold.

Mather retained a distinguished San Francisco architect, Charles Sumner Kaiser, to design the complex ("Kaiser," as a surname, was dropped when World War I broke out). Sumner's concept would set a precedent for the kind of architecture that Mather wanted in the parks: rustic in character, made of natural materials to harmonize with the environment, with form and design that alluded to frontier and alpine traditions.

The Rangers' Club illustrates Mather's personal commitment to an architectural esthetic appropriate for the national parks. Built in the summer of 1920, it has a distinctive U-shape plan and steeply pitched shake roofs. Massive peeled logs extending from the ground to the eaves along the exterior walls are shingled and stained dark brown, which, together with the massive granite chimney and multi-light windows and doors, afford the building a warm, domestic scale.

The interior of the Rangers' Club was arranged with common spaces on the first floor and bedrooms on the second floor. The first floor retains much of its original Arts & Crafts warmth—stout wooden furnishings, built-in bookcases with the added touch of jigsawn fir trees in the woodwork, and wagon-wheel chandeliers fringed with giant sequoia cones. In the living and dining rooms, chamfered columns support corbelled capitals, and exposed beams with chevron designs carry hand-hewn joists that contrast with a light-colored stain on the diagonal-patterned wood ceiling. Dark wooden wainscot paneling contrasts with the light plaster finish above and is used throughout the building. The ornamental designs of forest, alpine, and Native American cultural elements add rusticity to the space. A note on behalf of the occupants: This is a private residence, and visitors are reminded to respect their privacy.

To the east of the Rangers' Club is the garage/woodshed. It is L-shaped in plan and similar to the clubhouse, with steeply pitched gable roofs, shingle siding, and board-and-batten gable ends.

ADMINISTRATION BUILDING, POST OFFICE, AND MUSEUM

Mather's goal to relocate Yosemite Village took form following the completion of the Rangers' Club. During 1923, the National Park Service landscape staff at Yosemite submitted a master plan for an administration building, a post office, a museum, several concessioner studios and stores, and a hotel located on the north side of the Merced River. Although uses have changed and the buildings have been modified over the years, several retain those original qualities sought by Mather as compatible with the character of Yosemite Valley.

The major National Park Service buildings implementing Mather's plan—the Administration Building, Post Office, and Museum—have a unity in overall form and exterior materials. The three buildings have first-floor bases with battered-stone veneers that give the appearance of structural masonry, and projecting shingled upper stories trimmed with logs. A regular rhythm of window openings recessed into the lower walls conveys the massive nature of the battered-stone wall bases; upper-story windows are spaced and sized to preserve a large, shingled plane. Shallow-pitched, shingled gable roofs reinforce the long, low lines.

The designer first chosen for the Administration Building and the Post Office was Gilbert Stanley Underwood. Even though Underwood was to play an important role in designing future National Park Service and concessioner buildings, his Yosemite designs were rejected by the Washington-based Fine Arts Commission as inappropriate and too complex. Mather then turned to Los Angeles architect Myron Hunt. Hunt's concept for the new administration center buildings consisted of two-story structures with a horizontal emphasis that would blend with the granite cliffs behind the village.

Director Mather presided over the dedication of the new Administration Building and the laying of the Post Office and Museum cornerstones in November 1924. The Post Office, completed a year later, echoed the Administration Building's stone base and shingled-upper-story concept with minor variations: four large multi-light windows and three wide entrance bays on the south side, a porte cochere on the north side, and omission of log brackets and rafter ends.

In the early 1920s, the concept of national park museums was in the formative stages. The American Association of Museums, interested in the development of interpretive facilities, hired architect Herbert Maier to prepare a design proposal for Yosemite. The Laura Spelman Rockefeller Foundation responded with a sizable grant ($75,000), and construction began in 1925.

Maier followed the concepts of the other administration area buildings by designing a long, low, two-story building with a stone base and shingled upper story. He successfully subordinated the design to the setting and wrote, "To attempt attitudinal impressiveness here in a building would have meant entering into competition with the cliffs; and for such competition the architect has no stomach. The horizontal key, on the other hand, makes the museum blend easily into the flat ground." With further support from the Rockefeller Foundation, Maier went on to design other museums at Grand Canyon and Yellowstone, each with its own special interpretation of the setting.

The museum building, now only partially used for exhibit purposes, represents the early emphasis placed on interpretation of Yosemite's natural history. The Yosemite Museum Association, founded in 1920, was one of the first organizations in the national parks to support research and interpretive activities. Later it became the Yosemite Association, and the museum served as its center for collection and preservation of cultural artifacts, emphasizing Native American prehistory and history in the Yosemite region. Now known as the Valley District Building, exhibit functions were restored in 1976 with an Indian Cultural Center, and in 1988 an art gallery opened.

CONCESSIONER'S STUDIOS—
POHONO AND THE ANSEL ADAMS GALLERY

When the old village was relocated, the move included studios that had been owned by photographers and artists, some of whom had catered to Yosemite visitors since its earliest years. Two of those established around the turn of the century were given sites in the new village in 1925. Julius Boysen's Pohono Indian Studio has recently been restored to its original condition, and the massive peeled-log framed structure with shingle infill panels is now used as a wilderness center.

The other studio relocated from the old village is a complex of several buildings now operated as the Ansel Adams Gallery. Artist Harry Cassie Best opened a studio in the old village in 1902, which was destroyed by heavy snow loads in 1921 and rebuilt two years later. Plans for the new Best's Studio were incorporated into the relocated village, and construction was completed in 1926. The main building shows rustic features—battered stone piers, simple post-and-beam construction, and shallow-pitched roofs. The studio was designed to blend into its setting by the use of granite in the foundations, fireplace, and massive columns that embrace the dark-stained structure.

Harry Cassie Best established a reputation as a painter of western landscapes, and from his studio he sold his paintings, along with arts and crafts, curios, and photographs. At the time of his death in 1936, ownership and management of the studio passed to his daughter, Virginia, and her husband, Ansel Adams. In 1972 Best's Studio was renamed the Ansel Adams Gallery.

ANSEL ADAMS

Born in San Francisco in 1902, Adams manifested an early interest in music and the piano, which he initially hoped to develop into a professional career. He first visited Yosemite as a teenager, an experience of such intensity that he was to view it as a lifelong inspiration. He returned during the summers, and became caretaker of LeConte Memorial Lodge when he was twenty. These trips involved exploration, climbing and photography. While working there, he studied the many moods and climates of the valley and the Sierra high country and developed an interest in conservation. By 1920 he had formed an association with the Sierra Club. He studied photography with a photofinisher, producing early work influenced by the then-prevalent pictorialist style. Adams's extraordinary photographs carried on the legacy of Carleton Watkins and William Henry Jackson.

He began a gallery in San Francisco in 1933, the Ansel Adams Gallery. The first of his books dealing with the mastery of photographic technique, *Making a Photograph*, was published in 1935. During 1936–37 Adams moved into Yosemite Valley and made trips throughout the Southwest with Edward Weston, Georgia O'Keeffe, and David McAlpin. Having met Beaumont and Nancy Newhall in New York in 1939, the following year Adams, along with McAlpin, assisted in the foundation of the Department of Photography at the New York City Museum of Modern Art (MoMA).

Until his death in 1984, a long and prolific career created a body of work that has come to exemplify not only the purist approach to photography but, to many people, the definitive pictorial statement on the American western landscape. His Yosemite photographs capture memorable images of the Park's many moods.

THE AHWAHNEE HOTEL

Stephen Mather was chagrined to hear that Lady Astor refused to stay in the park because of the crude lodgings. She symbolized Mather's need for good accommodations for influential visitors who could support the park and the National Park Service. Concerned about the competing concession interests that created a tawdry appearance in the valley, he forced a merger of competing Yosemite concessioners capable of investing in large-scale projects, thus forming the Yosemite Park and Curry Company. Investing $200,000, he demanded construction of a new, fireproof luxury hotel capable of year-round operation. Gilbert Stanley Underwood was the recommended architect.

The owners desired a large hotel with one hundred guest rooms and a dining room for one thousand, but required that it be unobtrusive and take advantage of the magnificent views. The site is a deep, grassy meadow at the base of the Royal Arches. The hotel later used the Miwok Indian name for the valley they called *Ah-wah-ni* ("big mouth" or "the place of the big mouth"). Located at the east end of the valley, it is surrounded by a forest of black oak and Douglas fir, which provides seclusion from nearby development. Underwood knew that his building could not compete with the setting. He devised an asymmetrical plan with three wings, each three stories high, radiating out from a six-story central tower. The plan afforded good views of the dramatic scenery from every window.

Emphasized by green slate hip roofs, the horizontal sweep of the balconies and terraces at Ahwahnee provides visual interest on the exterior and varied spatial experiences on the interior. Massive granite-boulder piers and chimneys match the cliff walls and soar vertically throughout the complex. Broadened at their bases, the piers cast the first-floor window openings into deep shadow.

The fireproof design required a structural steel frame encased in concrete. What appears as rough-cut siding is really board-formed concrete stained the color of redwood. The exposed stone received similar care in detailing. Specifications required that the native granite "be laid with the natural weathered surface exposed and no freshly cut surfaces will be allowed for exterior exposure" and "the largest stone at the bottom gradually reducing the size of the stone to the top." The only part of the structure that is not fireproof is the dining room. Here, Underwood repeated a scheme from his other designs, supporting wooden trusses on paired log columns under a

12a The Ahwahnee Hotel

wooden roof; steel columns were bolted between the log columns, one on the interior of the building, one on the exterior.

The Y-shaped ground floor pivots around the elevator lobby. Underwood deftly created a succession of public spaces beginning at the far corner of the plan, leading from a porte cochere entrance through a log-and-stone entrance. Decorative Indian patterns with strong Art Deco influences predominate over a mixture of rustic and exotic interior motifs. The two-story lobby, delineated by plastered concrete columns, is set off by bands of French doors that open onto the landscape. The floor is decorated with earth-tone rubber tiles, and the cornice is stenciled in Indian designs. The unique lighting—triangular wrought-iron chandeliers and wall sconces—repeats designs used throughout the building.

Above the stately Grand Lounge (77-by-51-foot floor space), exposed concrete beams and joists arranged in a coffered pattern are painted to resemble timbers and decorated with bands of angular Indian patterns. Akin to a cathedral floor plan, the "nave" is graced by a twenty-four-foot-high window opening with five-by-six-foot stained-glass panels at the top. Intimate seating arrangements with easy chairs, soft couches, and low wooden tables with oversized ceramic lamps make the space inviting. Patterned drapes and Indian rugs on the polished oak floor add warmth. Enormous fireplaces made of cut sandstone face each other across the room. Above one hangs a kilim rug, above the other a De Stijl mural.

The small rooms off the "nave" of the Grand Lounge complete the cathedral plan of this wing. The "apse" is a solarium overlooking the southern meadow. One of the "transepts" is the California Room, with memorabilia from the gold rush days. The other is the Writing Room, featuring a wall-length oil painting on linen by Robert Boardman Howard depicting the flora and fauna of Yosemite Valley. Public spaces are also provided on mezzanine levels at each end.

The succession of public spaces is a prelude to one of the grandest rooms in any of the national parks, the 130-by-51-foot dining room. Light pours in from the 25-foot-high south-facing windows and from the alcove at the west end of the room, with triangular wrought-iron chandeliers and wall sconces provide warm light after dark. Over-scaled Indian patterns on the uppermost wall sections above the wood wainscoting are echoed in the linen curtains and on the china. Granite piers flank the alcove, framing splendid views of the valley and Yosemite Falls.

Underwood began designing the 150,000-square-foot building in 1925, and ground was broken the next summer. Construction was a logistical nightmare. Battles erupted between the contractor and architect about cost overruns, design changes, and schedules. Convoys of trucks bringing logs, stone, and concrete to the site traveled over marginally improved roads. Steel beams that were to be hauled in over the recently built road from Merced were judged to be too heavy for the new road, so the contractor had them cut into smaller lengths, that were later reconnected with plates.

As the interior began to take shape, the Yosemite Park and Curry Company hired Drs. Phyllis Ackerman and Arthur Upham Pope, experts in art history, to guide the interior decoration. They commissioned Jeanette Dyer Spencer to create stained-glass windows for the Grand Lounge and the basket-design mural for the elevator lobby, and Robert Boardman Howard to paint the mural for the Writing Room. They also personally chose the kilims and oriental rugs used in the interiors.

Ansel Adams was commissioned for promotional work for the hotel, and wrote,

■ "On entering the Ahwahnee one is conscious of calm and complete beauty echoing the mood of majesty and peace that is the essential quality of Yosemite. . . . Against a background of forest and precipice the architect had nestled the great structure of granite, scaling his design with sky and space and stone. To the interior all ornamentation has been confined, and therein lays a miracle of color and design. The Indian motif is supreme. . . . The designs are stylized with tasteful sophistication; decidedly Indian, yet decidedly more than Indian, they epitomize the involved and intricate symbolism of primitive man."

When the building opened on July 14, 1927, the consensus was that it was worth the wait. Stephen Mather's press release proclaimed: "The Ahwahnee is designed quite frankly for people who know the delights of luxurious living, and to whom the artistic and material comforts of their environment is important." Over the years, the Ahwahnee has greeted heads of state, from presidents to kings, as well as movie stars and international celebrities. But more important than the list of famous guests is the hotel's place in architectural history: it epitomizes the rustic ideal and embodies the aesthetic experience of Yosemite.

VALLEY BRIDGES

The approaches to the valley and the valley floor are threaded by the Merced River and its branches and by streams flowing from the cliffs. The South Fork of the Merced River and the Tuolumne River drainages add to the need for bridge crossings. Bridge building quickly followed the earliest access by tourists. The bridges are of timber, masonry, or concrete of single arches, or spans, or multiple arches. They are typically scaled to meet the expected traffic—foot and horse, and major or minor vehicle use. An aesthetic complement to the environment, the Yosemite bridges represent different eras of bridge builders and purposes.

The Wawona Covered Bridge, constructed on the South Fork of the Merced River in the southern part of the park, is Yosemite's oldest extant bridge. Built as an open-deck structure in 1868, it was converted to a covered bridge in 1878. Following a major flood in 1955 the bridge was dismantled and reconstructed in 1956 in Yosemite Pioneer History Center. Originally 118 feet long and 16 feet wide, modified timber Queen Post trusses braced by steel tie rods support the bridge.

Built under the U.S. Cavalry administration of Yosemite (1890–1914), several bridges, including three at the base of Bridalveil Falls, illustrate the development of a rustic-style method of construction. One- or two-arch spans of reinforced concrete have stone masonry walls applied to the concrete, and gravel fill to the roadway level.

Sentinel Bridge crossing the Merced River west of Yosemite Chapel was the first bridge constructed by the National Park Service. The three-span reinforced structure, built in 1919 and designed in an unornamental style, shed rustic features of granite veneer and decorative lamps.

The Ahwahnee, Clark's Bridge, Happy Isles, Pohono, Stoneman, Sugar Pine, and Yosemite Creek Bridges represent the National Park Service's prowess in coordinating landscape design with rustic-design character. The bridges were built during the mid-1920s to 1930s, and National Park Service landscape architect Thomas Vint worked on the designs under the supervision of the U.S. Bureau of Public Roads. Construction of the single- and multi-arch spans proceeded with erection of timber falsework for the laying of hand-cut local-granite arch ring stones (voussoirs) and facings; the stone veneer served as part of the formwork for the reinforced-concrete arch and spandrel structure. The El Capitan Bridge crossing the Merced and Tioga Road Bridge near Tuolumne Meadow is a National Park Service–designed multi-span bridge of steel and concrete structure on stone abutments and piers. Large redwood logs, sidewalk stringers and beam-ends, and, originally, log guardrails maintain a rustic character with a horizontal line compatible to the surrounding flat terrain.

12b The Tioga Road—
Tuolumne Meadows and the High Country

Leaving Yosemite Valley via the Big Oak Flat Road to Crane Flat, the Tioga Road (California Highway 120 outside the park) begins climbing to an elevation of 9,914 feet, exiting the park's eastern side at the Tioga Pass entrance.

WHITE WOLF LODGE

The Lodge complex of the main building with dining room, store, cabins, and tent platforms with canvas tents is a starting point for hikers or mountaineers going into the high country. The simple, white-clapboard-frame main-lodge building with a broad porch, a replacement of the original lodge that collapsed under heavy snows in 1969, is a lingering example of Yosemite's early visitor accommodations. Originally a residence in the center of a lush meadow used for summer pasturage, the lodge opened in 1926 to serve the increasing traffic on the Tioga Road. The tent platforms, cabins, and nearby campgrounds were added as improved roads attracted more travelers to Tuolumne Meadows.

PARSONS MEMORIAL LODGE

Soda Springs has been a landmark and favorite camping site since the earliest travelers came to Yosemite. Using Soda Springs as a base, the Sierra Club organized their first outings in the Tuolumne Meadows area in 1901. They acquired 160 acres to protect the springs and provide access into the high country. When Sierra Club director Edward Taylor Parsons died, a memorial fund was established for a single-room building with a fireplace to serve as headquarters and a meeting place; it was constructed in 1915.

Parsons Memorial Lodge is a simple building: 1,040 square feet, symmetrical, and rectangular. Some uncertainty exists about who designed the lodge—Bernard Maybeck or his brother-in-law, John White. Perhaps they both collaborated with structural engineer Walter Huber. Maybeck's design values, stressing harmony with the landscape, are expressed in the use of local pink feldspar granite, peeled logs, a low-rise shed roof, and many hand-crafted touches.

The rubble-stone masonry walls, deep door and window openings, and shallow-pitched roof visually tie the building to the contours of the nearby granite peaks. The stone walls, battered from three feet thick at the base to two feet at the eaves, are laid on a concrete core. The Roman arch at the south entrance frames a sturdy arched door of heavy planks bound with wrought-iron straps. The voussoirs are dressed, as are the lintel and jamb stones throughout the building. All the windows are protected by shutters, heavily studded with nails to make them bear-proof. The massive stone chimney rises above the roofline into a gentle, flat-topped arch.

The lodge's interior is an open space with exposed stone walls and a peeled-log roof. The stone fireplace on the north wall provides a focus point on summer evenings. Stone benches under the windows have thick wooden-plank seats. Diagonal log braces on both the interior and exterior rest on low stone buttresses on the east and west walls. Rafters, 1 $\frac{1}{2}$ feet in diameter and flattened on top, carry a roof made of peeled logs six to nine inches in diameter with rafter outlookers projecting two feet beyond the roof's edge.

TUOLUMNE MEADOWS AND TIOGA PASS

In the early 1930s the National Park Service expanded services at Tuolumne Meadows and the Tioga Pass Entrance Station. In rapid succession, a ranger station, campgrounds, comfort station, and visitor center were constructed at the meadows. The Civilian Conservation Corps added manpower to the construction crews in 1933 and increased the number of buildings in the area over the next few years.

Beginning with the entrance station in 1931, the buildings represent studied examples of the National Park Service's rustic style. National Park Service landscape architect John Wosky was assigned to Yosemite and began designing the stone and timber buildings in the Tioga Pass–Tuolumne Meadows area. The buildings carry a consistent rustic theme in the use of heavy ashlar-patterned granite graded in size from foundation to eave, log-roof framing extended at the eaves, a variety of plank and board-and-batten siding, and shake-shingled roofs.

The original visitor center, built in 1934, is a small, one-story rectangular building with a porch across the front. A low-pitched gable roof with shake shingles is carried on stone piers matching the bold, rugged appearance of roughly coursed, ashlar-patterned granite side walls and chimney. The "new" Visitor Center, originally built as a mess hall, has typical intersecting gabled forms, a steeply pitched roof, and stone base. Paired peeled-log columns at the entrance patio and projecting whittle-end log rafters represent the best of rustic detailing. Planked siding runs in a horizontal lower band, moves into vertical board-and-batten from window sills to eaves, and returns to horizontal at the eaves.

The comfort stations relate to the local geology with the use of heavy masonry walls. The shingled roof with jerkinhead ends rests on massive, battered granite walls. Projecting timber rafters support the roof structure.

The Tuolumne Meadows Ranger Station is an L-shaped structure with a steeply pitched roof. The exposed frame of peeled logs on a stone foundation is infilled with vertical wood siding. Peeled-log rafters project at roof eaves. The Ranger's Residence is a two-story wood-frame structure with steeply pitched shake-shingle roofs. The finely crafted rustic dwelling has an open porch along one side with paired peeled-log columns supporting the roof eaves with whittle-end projecting log rafters. Exterior plank walls are similar in treatment to the old Mess Hall.

TIOGA PASS ENTRANCE STATION

The entrance station at Tioga Pass is a highly refined National Park Service version of checking stations to control traffic and to portray the unique character of a national park to the traveler. National Park Service's *Park & Recreation Structures* (1938) heralded the design as "an entrance way of simple stone pylons and pivoting gates guarded by a ranger's house of compact plan. The 'whittled' rafter ends are interesting. The difficulties inherent in boulder masonry are here met better than usual." A modest acknowledgment for a superbly designed and scaled structure.

The shallow-pitched roof of shake shingles extends downward to form a porch, supported by peeled-log columns and stone pillars, and the gable-roof pitch parallels the ground and flows into the entrance gate pylon. The rustic log gate constructed in 1999 is a replica of the original.

12b Tioga Pass Entrance Station

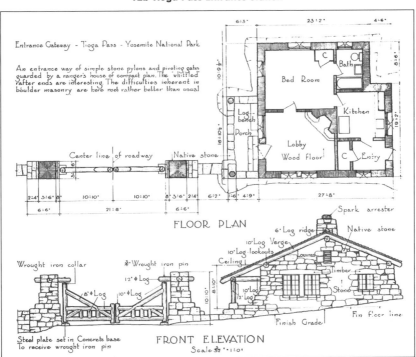

Entrance Gateway - Tioga Pass - Yosemite National Park

An entrance way of simple stone pylons and pivoting gates guarded by a ranger's house of compact plan. The whittled rafter ends are interesting. The difficulties inherent in boulder masonry are here met rather better than usual.

FLOOR PLAN

FRONT ELEVATION

Scale ½" = 1'-0"

12c The Wawona Road

The Wawona Road (California Highway 41 outside the park) leaves Yosemite Valley from the junction near Bridalveil Falls and climbs to the Wawona Tunnel and Discovery Viewpoint. From the tunnel, the road climbs to Chinquapin Point, links up with the Wawona Road at more than 6,000-feet elevation, descends past Wawona, the Yosemite Pioneer History Center, and Mariposa Grove, then exits at the park's south entrance.

BADGER PASS SKI AREA

The earliest residents in Yosemite Valley cultivated winter sports to help them through the long cold season when they were isolated from the rest of the world. Skating areas were shaped from frozen rivers and ponds. Completion of the Yosemite Valley Railroad in 1907 made Yosemite Valley accessible to tourists in the winter. When the all-year highway was opened in 1926, Yosemite became more accessible for winter activities. In 1929 Yosemite made a strong bid for the 1932 Olympics. Ironically, Lake Placid was chosen instead but was forced to truck in snow due to a light winter, while Yosemite was groaning with just under twelve feet of snow along Glacier Point Road.

After lengthy discussions about appropriate winter use in Yosemite, including a debate over whether that use would be cross-country or downhill skiing, the Yosemite Park and Curry Company received National Park Service approval in 1935 for a downhill ski area at Monroe Meadows. Although this meant intensive use and a whole new type of structure, the only National Park Service guidelines were these: "New facilities for winter sports use . . . should not be built until provision is made for their proper maintenance and supervision."

Architect Eldridge (Ted) Spencer designed the project, which included a lodge and ski lift; the lodge opened in December 1935. A simple Swiss-chalet character is implied from a shallow-pitched shed roof over the entire building. Dressed timbers, exposed over the lounge, form trusses that support the roof and heavy snow loads. French doors open from the lounge onto a broad terrace, and a second floor provides access to a balcony that faces the ski area. A wide overhang supported by truss extensions, along with the balcony and terrace, add to the chalet's character. The original furnishings, decorations, and artwork follow Nordic skiing themes.

12c The Wawona Hotel

THE WAWONA HOTEL

The Wawona Hotel is the oldest resort complex in the National Park System. Unlike park hotels built by the railroaders, the complex began as a stagecoach stop in 1859 on a passenger and freight line. The first Wawona Hotel building opened in 1876. Passengers going from Mariposa Grove to Yosemite Valley paused for rest and refreshment at the Victorian resort. Today's charming, seven-building complex of two-story white clapboard structures with porches, verandahs, and Victorian trim recall an earlier era of travel that offers a quiet reflective setting after the titanic drama of Yosemite Valley.

The complex is on the edge of a rolling hill that overlooks Wawona Meadow and a nine-hole golf course. A circular drive with a centered cobblestone fountain leads to the main building. To the side of the drive is landscape painter Thomas Hill's studio, built around 1886. A small balustrade simulating a widow's walk crowns the steeply pitched shake roof. The slender picket railing and upper brackets recall the delicate filigrees of the perpendicular Eastlake style. After the artist's death in 1908, the building passed through a variety of uses, including ice cream parlor, dance hall, and recreation room. It has been restored as a museum.

Constructed over a period of forty years, the architecture is of less interest than the integrity of the whole complex. Unity is achieved through formal placement of the buildings on the rural landscape, by the principal building material, and by form and massing and color. The porches and verandahs around all the buildings further unite them and encourage an airy connection with the landscape. The buildings share other common elements, such as the cornice returns on Washburn Cottage. Stick style and Eastlake details appear in porch railings and column brackets. Even Palladian classical elements can be seen, as in the cupola of Moore Cottage.

The earliest hotel on the site was a small log cabin built by Yosemite pioneer Galen. Clark in 1859. Moving from a cabin at another location, he expanded a small settlement into Clark's Station and later adopted the name Big Tree Station for the stagecoach stop. When the Grove was ceded to California as part of the 1864 grant, Clark was appointed guardian. His tasks distracted him from running his hotel, and a partnership headed by Henry Washburn, a Merced stage-line operator, acquired his holdings in 1870. For the next sixty years, the Washburn family provided hospitality at Wawona Meadows.

Henry Washburn was a Vermonter, and his New England heritage is evident in the buildings he erected. His first lodgings for guests, Long White (now called Clark Cottage), was built in 1876. A fire two years later destroyed the original Galen Clark stage-stop buildings, but Long White survived to become the anchor for the new Wawona Hotel complex. In 1882 a Washburn daughter, Jean, suggested the Indian word *Wah-wo-nah* ("guardian spirit and deity of the Big Trees") as a more fitting name for the hotel complex than Big Tree Station. Today the big block letters HOTEL WAWONA stand out on the building's upper wall, greeting guests as they have for more than a century.

The main hotel building opened in 1879. The T-shaped plan has a main section, 32 by 140 feet, with public spaces on the ground floor and an employee dormitory on the second floor. The nearly symmetrical front elevation appears as two stories of deep porches with a verandah roof surrounding the building under a main hip roof. Porch railings are in a simple pattern of rectangles. Interiors depict a Victorian character with period furnishings (not original), blocked wallpaper, and light fixtures dating from 1917.

Moore Cottage, picturesquely sited on a knoll behind the main hotel building, is an elegant guest house favored by honeymooners. Built in 1896 the cottage is rich in form and details. It is designed in three equally proportioned horizontal tiers—a first-floor porch, a steep hip roof pierced by oversize dormers, and a cupola with a Palladian window. Gable ends in the dormer ends are filled with diamond-patterned shingles. On the verandah, fretwork railings between chamfered posts and gingerbread brackets of diagonal pendant diamonds and scrollwork add a touch of grace.

The Manager's Residence, small and L-shaped, was completed in 1884 and is now known as Little White. It is a single-story, wood-frame structure with a verandah wrapping around the building; the verandah and main roof are covered with wooden shakes. Aligned with the adjacent Clark Cottage, the residence repeats the New England arrangement of gabled roof, white clapboards, and a verandah with evenly spaced columns.

The Annex, constructed in 1917–18, is a long, rectangular building with thirty-seven rooms and shared baths. A two-story verandah around the building is covered by an extension of the main shake-shingled roof. A simple railing of vertical balustrades and T-shaped diagonal railings give the building a Stick-style appearance. The west end contains a sun parlor on the first floor, overlooking the golf course.

PIONEER VILLAGE

A collection of furnished historic buildings, most of them relocated from their original settings elsewhere in the park, and horse-drawn coaches and wagons are displayed at the Pioneer Yosemite History Center. Buildings vary in form, materials, and function. The 1876 Anderson Cabin is typical of several early settler log cabins. A cabin (1904) and a tack room (1917) represent the U.S. Army's stewardship of the park. The Jorgensen Studio (1904) of peeled logs was relocated from Yosemite Village. The Crane Flat Ranger Cabin (1900) is a log cabin representative of structures replaced by the National Park Service. An example of early control of Yosemite troublemakers is the stone jail, ten feet square with eighteen-inch-thick walls and a shallow wood-frame hipped roof. The exposed peeled-log structural frame of the Wells Fargo Office (1912), infilled with decorative patterns of log, suggests a Swiss chalet character.

1 Crater Lake National Park

Section

Oregon**2**

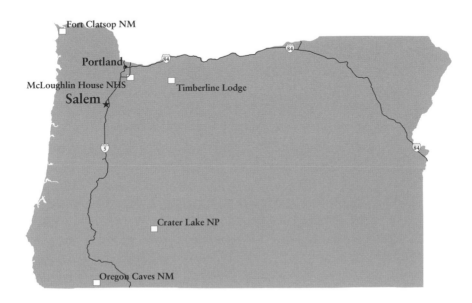

Fort Clatsop NM

Portland

McLoughlin House NHS

Salem

Timberline Lodge

Crater Lake NP

Oregon Caves NM

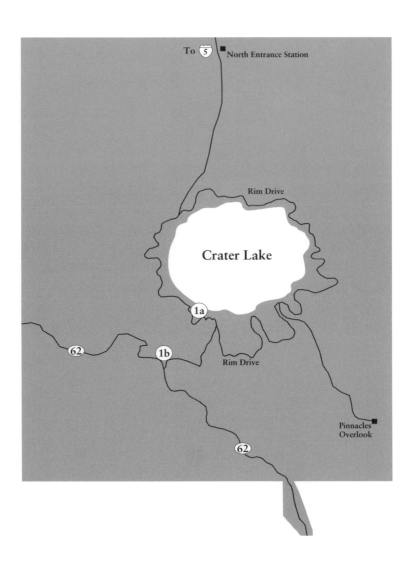

To ⑤ ■ North Entrance Station

Rim Drive

Crater Lake

1a

62 1b

Rim Drive

Pinnacles
Overlook

62

1 Crater Lake National Park
Klamath County, Oregon
www.nps.gov/crla

The park is located in south-central Oregon on Highway 62, sixty miles northwest of Klamath Falls and eighty miles northwest of Medford. The north entrance and thirty-three-mile Rim Drive are closed from mid-October to late June.

■ "The eye beholds twenty miles of unbroken cliffs ranging from five hundred to two thousand feet in height, encircling a deep sheet of placid water in which the mirrored walls vie with the originals in brilliancy and greatly enhance the depth of the prospect. Although the blue of the lake is deeper than anyone who has not beheld it can imagine, it is yet so transparent that even on a hazy day a white dinner plate ten inches in diameter may be seen at a depth of nearly one hundred feet."

Gilbert H. Grosvenor, *National Geographic Magazine*

A long drive through the Oregon portion of the Cascade Range offers views of many volcanic peaks—Mounts Hood, Jefferson, Washington, Three Sisters, Bachelor, and McLoughlin. At the south end of the range, a truncated cone (the remains of Mount Mazama) holds a 1,958-foot-deep caldera filled with the waters of a magnificent lake as intensely blue as the Oregon sky on a clear day: Crater Lake.

Surrounding the lake is a rim of steep jagged cliffs rising as high as two thousand feet. The uptilt of the volcanic cone and the rim conceals the lake until the visitor reaches the edge of the cliffs. Even under sunny summer skies, traces of winter's heavy snows fill crevices down to the lake's surface. The extraordinary vivid blue of Crater Lake results from the water's purity; it contains almost no organic matter and few dissolved minerals.

Crater Lake has astonished visitors since a party of gold prospectors led by John Westey Hillman first accidentally "discovered" it in 1853 while searching for the Lost Cabin gold mine. Over the years, occasional tourists visited but it remained unexploited until Judge William Gladstone Steel arrived from Portland in 1885. In 1886 a U.S. Geological Survey team led by Captain Clarence Dutton hauled a twenty-six-foot boat, the *Cleetwood,* to the top of the mountain and lowered it over the steep cliffs into the water to map the lake and make soundings. Their soundings with piano wire set the lake's depth at 1,996 feet, a measurement close to that of sonar soundings taken in 2000 that measured the lake depth at 1,958 feet. After seventeen years of devoted struggle, Steel succeeded in having the lake set aside as a national park. President Theodore Roosevelt signed the enabling legislation in 1902, and Crater Lake became the nation's sixth national park. Two boundary changes expanded the park's original size of 160,000 acres to its current 183,000 acres.

WILLIAM GLADSTONE STEEL

There is a story that as a Kansas schoolboy Steel had read about the discovery of Crater Lake in a newspaper that was used to wrap his lunch. He became obsessed with the idea of seeing it in person. Years later he achieved his goal and saw that it was lovelier than he ever imagined. Steel described his feelings and reactions as he viewed the lake for the first time on August 15, 1885:

■ "Not a foot of the land about the lake had been touched or claimed. An overmastering conviction came to me that this wonderful spot must be saved, wild and beautiful, just as it was, for all future generations, and that it was up to me to do something. I then and there had the impression that in some way, I didn't know how, the lake ought to become a National Park. I was so burdened with the idea that I was distressed.

Many hours in Captain Dutton's tent, we talked of plans to save the lake from private exploitation. We discussed its wonders, mystery and inspiring beauty, its forests and strange lava structure. The captain agreed with the idea that something ought to be done—and done at once if the lake was to be saved, and that it should be made a National Park."

Steel acknowledged at a National Park conference in 1917 that Professor Joseph LeConte was present with him at the rim that day for counsel as to how to save Crater Lake "for the people of this great country." Steel reported that they discussed the problem at length and decided upon a national park.

Steel devoted the rest of his life and fortune to this great purpose and to care for the park after it was established. There were no fish in Crater Lake until 1888 when Steel carried pails of fingerling trout up the mountainside and down the rim. After Crater Lake National Park was established on May 14, 1902, Steel formed the Crater Lake Company in 1907 for the purpose of building a hotel, placing boats on the lake, and conducting a stage line to the park. He served as the park's second superintendent and later as a park commissioner until his death in 1934.

Early travelers endured a long journey to gaze over the rim at the fabulous, enchanting blue waters. The long distances from supply centers and heavy winter snowfall limited the development of tourist services. Building was difficult in the severe climate, which seemed to be divided into two seasons: a short but beautiful three-month summer and a long snowy winter. The yearly snowfall at Crater Lake averages fifty feet, and a record snowpack in April 1983 was measured at twenty-one feet.

Two historic districts of buildings and landscapes as well as the Rim Drive are noteworthy at Crater Lake. At the rim, Steel's vision evolved into a hotel overlooking the lake, Crater Lake Lodge. Nearby, the National Park Service built some of its earliest rustic-style buildings. As originally executed, the park's administrative center, a mile from the Rim Village at Munson Valley, contains one of the handsomest groups of rustic structures in the entire National Park System.

1a Rim Village

CRATER LAKE LODGE

In spite of its prime location, the original Crater Lake Lodge was disappointing in many respects. Compared to other national park concessioner-built lodges in the midst of sublime landscapes, such as Timberline Lodge at Mount Hood or Grand Canyon Lodge at the North Rim, Crater Lake Lodge lacks the special enrichment that could make it truly fitting—dramatic forms, for example, or appropriate exterior materials and special treatments for window and door openings. The original plans underestimated the heavy snow loads at Crater Lake's 7,100-foot elevation—which can measure up to sixty feet a season—and used construction techniques and materials better suited to lower elevations. In general, the workmanship was quite ordinary, and guests were not enthralled by the dreary double-loaded guest room corridors and unappealing rooms. Inadequate mechanical and electrical systems plagued hotel operations from the start, and the lack of sufficient exits and fire-safety precautions were gross oversights.

By the 1960s safety deficiencies, material deterioration, and structural dilapidation had far outpaced concessioners' improvements. The National Park Service acquired the building in 1967, and a decade later no one could deny that Crater Lake Lodge had clearly become a substandard hotel.

The National Park Service proposed alternatives calling for the removal and rehabilitation of Crater Lake Lodge. Much of the debate on the lodge's future centered on the condition of the lodge, the cost of restoration, and the environmental impact. The National Park Service, supported by the Oregon historic preservation community, nominated the lodge to the National Register of Historic Places, and interest in the historic building, which had been a favorite honeymoon destination for seventy years, resulted in a National Park Service plan in 1988 to save Crater Lake Lodge as part of the comprehensive Rim Village Redevelopment Plan. The plan was discarded after completion of the Lodge project in 1995 and was replaced by a 1998 visitor services plan.

Engineers contracted by the National Park Service monitored the structural integrity of the lodge through the 1980s. In the spring of 1989, just before the lodge was to open for the summer season, the engineers advised

1a Crater Lake Lodge

the park that the great hall wing was unsafe for occupants. This compelled the National Park Service to keep the lodge closed and begin a comprehensive rehabilitation project.

The plan to rehabilitate Crater Lake Lodge called for returning the exterior appearance and interior public areas to the character of great national park lodges of the 1920s. After two years of planning and design, construction work began in 1991. Some original materials, such as the masonry stones, were salvaged for reuse, but very little of the original building could be saved. The great hall wing was dismantled and rebuilt and most of the area was gutted. A steel structural support system, utilities, and life-safety systems meeting modern hotel standards were built into the new facility. Guest rooms were enlarged, lowering the total number of rooms from 105 to 71. Some interesting guestrooms were created by making use of the attic space as the upper level for two-story suites. The rehabilitation of Crater Lake Lodge was completed in fall 1994 at a cost of more than $15 million.

On May 20, 1995, Crater Lake Lodge reopened to the public. The extensive structural rebuilding, replacement of mechanical and electrical systems, installation of new finishes and elevators, and additional exits and safety devices make the lodge a safe and attractive accommodation. For the first time since its original opening, Crater Lake Lodge was a project finally completed.

The decision to maintain a lodge at the rim of Crater Lake will remain controversial. The State Historic Preservation Office is considering removing the structure from its list of historic structures because less than 10 percent of the original fabric remains in place. However, the efforts made by the National Park Service to retain the building's historic exterior appearance and to restore the interiors to a 1920s eclectic rustic style should be appreciated in the context of the safety and comfort provided for guests at this historic cultural resource.

NATIONAL PARK SERVICE BUILDINGS AT THE RIM VILLAGE

Several National Park Service buildings at the Rim Village showcase the evolving rustic style. The buildings were not planned as a model "village." They are a mixture of concessioner- and National Park Service–built structures unified by the landscape, designed and implemented by Merel Sager and Francis Lange in the late 1920s and '30s under the direction of Thomas Vint, based in the National Park Service's Western Field Office in San Francisco. Unity is achieved through the limited selection of building materials—stone, wood siding stained dark brown to contrast with white window frames, steeply pitched shake roofs and the promenade that ties the site together. An effort to achieve harmony within the site is evident in the use of local materials and the choice of designs suited to the harsh environment.

Rim Village Visitor Center

Fred Kiser, a nationally recognized scenic artist known for his hand-colored photographs, built this structure in 1921 to serve as his southern Oregon headquarters, studio, and salesroom for his work and photographic supplies. Kiser had his design and built a one-story, rectangular, stone-and-wood structure near the edge of the caldera wall west of Crater Lake Lodge and in front of the park's most popular viewpoint, an outcrop called Victor Rock. Uncoursed local boulders faced on a concrete foundation, horizontal lap siding, board and batten in gable ends, and steeply pitched shake-shingle roofs were incorporated into the addition to match the original building. Gable detailing—a plank bargeboard flush with the roof edge and siding—suggests a veneered frame structure. Wood shingles covered the gable roofs of both the original section and the addition of 1926, and overhanging eaves were supported by exposed, peeled-log purlins. Multipaned sliding windows were used on all levels of the studio. The south façade had a simple peeled-log pergola over the entry. A more elaborate pergola, rustic in character with peeled-log supports resting on stone piers on a stone terrace, was added early to the building's north elevation, enhancing a visitor's entry experience.

The National Park Service converted the building into an information office in 1930 when Kiser went broke, then called it an exhibit building, and finally the Rim Village Visitor Center. Alterations to the Kiser studio included removal of the pergolas in the 1930s, covering of the log purlins, replacement and removal of some of the original windows, and replacement of the original sheathing with horizontal board siding. A restoration project in 2000 restored some of the original windows and siding features.

Community House

The Community House was originally built to provide park visitors with a place for evening activities and informal gatherings, due to its proximity to the old Rim Campground. It has also served as a headquarters for park naturalists and a museum. Erected in 1924 and based on National Park Service architects' designs, the Community House is a one-story, rectangular, wood-framed structure set against a backdrop of mature evergreens in the northwest corner of the former campground. Original rustic elements modified over the years are a shingle exterior, a porch and supporting columns, and an entrance door. The massive battered wall on the east elevation is built of random-coursed boulders. A 2000 construction restored some of the original features.

Cafeteria Building

In 1928 the concessioner completed the latest addition to Rim Village, a cafeteria and supply store. Applying National Park Service designs, the Crater Lake National Park Company erected a stone and wood-frame building—one and a half stories in height, rectangular in plan, with a service wing on the south side of the building, and situated several hundred feet south of the caldera edge, oriented toward the lake. Stones similar in size and color to those used in the Kiser Studio were used in the building's exterior walls. Board-and-batten siding was used above on the gable ends, and the steeply pitched roof was covered with wood shingles. At the visitor entrance, a recessed central entry with peeled-log columns flanks two pairs of multipaned casement windows. Other multipaned windows placed throughout the structure further punctuate the building's stone and wood surfaces. The cafeteria retained its historic appearance until 1955 when a ski-warming hut was added. The addition was followed by a series of other extensions in 1968 and 1971 that increased the size of the original building threefold.

Sinnott Memorial

The Sinnott Memorial was constructed in 1930 under the supervision of the National Park Service's Landscape Division and named as a memorial to an Oregon congressman. It was conceived by John C. Merriam and designed by Merel Sager. Merriam named it Observation Point No. 1, where visitors were to receive an orientation of the park's geology at the parapet and through the museum's exhibits, then go out and see the beauty of the park through the boat tour or along Rim Drive, which featured observation stations located at places of especially fine views. It was the first structure in the park to use massive stone-masonry construction and was considered an excellent example of the rustic style, setting the tone for all future National Park Service structures in the park.

The irregularly shaped, stone-and-concrete structure with a log-framed roof is built into a rock outcrop on the slope of the caldera, about fifty feet below the rim. Access to the building is by a moderately steep walkway with steps. The building is entered through an elliptically shaped "observation room" on the north side of the structure. A thirty-inch-tall stone parapet below a large opening offers unobstructed views of the lake. Exterior walls are uncoursed load-bearing native stone on a reinforced concrete foundation, pierced on the east side by a square window opening and a door leading from the museum to the exterior stairs (shielded from view by a massive stone wall). Double-glazed, tongue-and-groove doors are located on the west side of the observation room. A stone parapet wall that extends out from the exterior walls guards the open observation platform. A museum is located along the interior walls.

Comfort Stations

Designed and built by the National Park Service from 1930 to 1937 following rustic-design principles employed elsewhere at the Rim Village, the

1a Staff Housing at Government Camp, 1931

1b Munson Valley Administration Building and Dormitory, 1936; detail (p. 131)

Comfort Stations are typically simple one-story wood-framed buildings with steeply pitched, shake-shingle roofs. Built in 1938, the Plaza Comfort Station near the cafeteria, provides an opportunity to inspect construction techniques of boulder masonry and infill planking siding, and board-and-batten walls like the ones used at the Park Headquarters at Munson Valley. It is a superb example of a veneer of massive uncoursed boulders battered from the foundation to the eaves at the building's corners, integrating the stone and wood infill walls. There is another comfort station behind the cafeteria designed by Merel Sager and built in 1930.

The Watchman Lookout is also on the National Register of Historic Places and successfully displays the ideas of rustic architecture. A rehabilitation project began in 1999 to restore its original features.

1b Munson Valley Park Headquarters

About three miles north of the Annie Springs entrance, the road passes Munson Valley Park Headquarters. This was the site selected for one of the most comprehensive Rustic architectural programs ever undertaken by the National Park Service. Landscape architect Merel Sager was assigned the task of laying out the administrative, residential, and maintenance facilities and establishing design guidelines. The administrative core included an administration building and a ranger dormitory forming two sides of a plaza. The rustic character of the residential buildings was carried out through a sequence of small stone-and-timber cottages that become progressively larger, culminating in the large Superintendent's Residence on the hill. The residential and maintenance areas are tucked out of view in the valley's trees.

The National Park Service Landscape Division designers set out to achieve high-quality, nonintrusive rustic design in all the planned structures. Buildings are situated at the edge of the meadow and forest following the contours of the land, and profiles were kept horizontal and low. Sager was especially conscious of the dramatic setting, overscaling many architectural features accordingly. In response to the local climate and geology, he chose massive stone masonry and steeply pitched roofs as the central theme. Native materials and natural colors were used, and severely straight lines were avoided to portray a craftsman quality.

1a Rim Village Comfort Station

Sager continued his experiments with stone walls of unprecedented size, which had begun with the Sinnott Memorial and Comfort Stations at the Rim Village. A unique construction method was devised in order to achieve the desired rustic effect for the one-and-a-half-story buildings in Munson Valley in a short building season. The construction sequence started with heavy wooden-formwork framing for the concrete-and-stone foundation walls that outlined the interior surface of the exterior walls. The forms braced the wooden framing of the second floor and roof. Next, massive boulders, two to three feet in diameter and some as large as five feet across, were forced into place as work progressed on the upper wood framing. A space of several inches was left between the masonry and formwork, and was later filled with concrete. Finally, as the masonry walls reached the eaves and after the concrete was sufficiently cured, the formwork was removed and the weight of the second floor was transferred to the masonry walls.

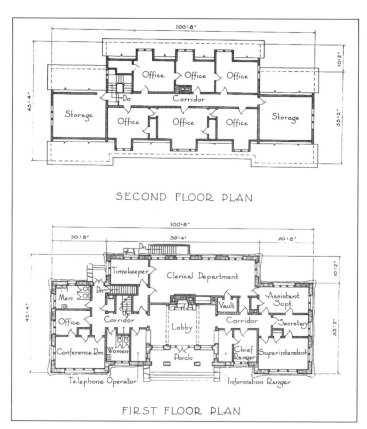

SECOND FLOOR PLAN

FIRST FLOOR PLAN

1b Administration Building

1b Administration Building, 1936

The battered stonework retains a strong visual tie to the steeply pitched gable roofs that express the high degree of design sensitivity. The intersecting roofs and gable and shed dormers of asymmetrical buildings were covered with wooden shakes placed in a staggered hit-or-miss pattern to give a textured appearance; symmetrical buildings received straight courses of shakes. Gable ends were finished with vertical board-and-batten siding. The eaves detailing on the projecting gable ends adds a finely finished touch to the building; bargeboards are pierced purlins, giving the buildings a tightly constructed feeling.

The Administration Building is a fine example of how a building can be merged into the landscape. Although prominent in the grouping because of its size, the design makes allowance for the building site, as well as for materials and how they must respond to the local climate and geology. Masterful handling of the two-story building's massing is a tour de force of rustic design. A steeply pitched, shake-shingle roof caps a one-story base of massive uncoursed boulders with deeply recessed entrance and window openings. Two symmetrical wings, with roof ridges lower than the central main roof, create

143

1b Administration Building

the building's form. Dormers piercing the central roof provide second-floor space, a sensitive manipulation of the floor plan to preserve the dominant form and character of a sheltering roof.

The Superintendent's Residence, a National Historic Landmark, and the Ranger Dormitory, now serving as a visitor center contact station with offices, called for a compact floor plan because of the unique construction method employed in the Munson Valley Administration Buildings. The two-story structures employed the same massing and materials used in the Administration Building. Massive local boulders, steeply pitched shake-shingle roofs, and deeply recessed window openings were repeated in the build-

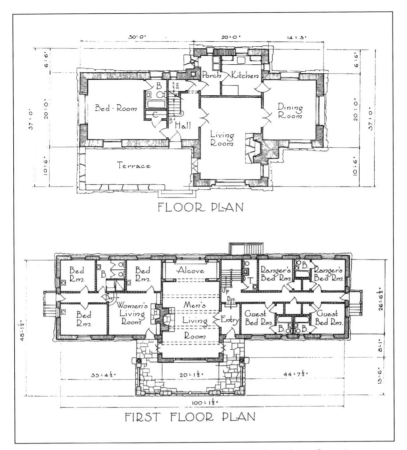

FLOOR PLAN

FIRST FLOOR PLAN

1b Superintendent's Residence (upper) and Ranger Dormitory (lower)

ings. Similarly shaped boulders were carefully graduated in size from foundations to plates for the battered exterior walls. The housing carried exterior themes into the interior, where the buildings were finished with fine woodwork detailing, Mission-style furniture, wrought-iron light fixtures, and stone fireplaces. The interiors of the Administration and Residential Buildings were finished with wall planking, wrought-iron light fixtures, and stone fireplaces. Some of the period furnishings are still in place. A maintenance complex includes a mess hall, warehouse, and several support buildings, all executed with similar rustic design and construction features.

The National Park Service Landscape Division succeeded in conceiving and implementing a superb complex admirably suited to location and climate. The geology of the area is reflected in the stone building "bases." The stone-and-concrete lower walls are perfect for the wet cold climate where rot and the pressure of deep snows easily destroy less substantial buildings. The thick stone walls provide insulation as well as protection against severe weather. Verticality was emphasized to emulate the steep terrain and coniferous forest. The ingenious construction methods enabled completion of several building exteriors in one summer.

In sparse complimentary language, the National Park Service's *Park and Recreation Structure* (1939) described the design concept's superb quality of nonintrusive character, stating, "Unifying, well-defined structural traits persist. Steep roof pitch, dictated by the heavy snowfalls in the latitude here, and masonry employing boulders of impressive size, combined with rough-sawn or vertical boards and battens, are chief among the factors common to all."

Overall, the complex is an architectural jewel endowed with a special identity from the past. The National Park Service addressed the toll taken by time and building modifications with a major rehabilitation program in the 1980s and '90s that won design awards for sensitive adaptive work, including the addition of building entrance snow tunnels used temporarily for "office" buildings. Design of the complex originally accommodated the staff in summer months, who then moved to Medford in the winter. The adaptive rehabilitation work was done to accommodate the year-round occupancy with design sensitivity and elimination of previous modifications. A major rehabilitation is planned for the Superintendent's Residence.

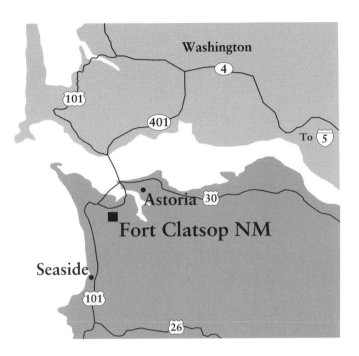

2 Fort Clatsop National Memorial
Astoria, Clatsop County, Oregon
www.nps.gov/focl

Fort Clatsop is located in the northernmost corner of Oregon near the mouth of the Columbia River, about five miles southwest of Astoria, Oregon, off U.S. 101. From Highway 101 turn east onto Business Loop 101, then follow the signs about three miles to Fort Clatsop. From the south, follow Route 101 for twelve miles north of Seaside, then follow the signs along Route 101 to Fort Clatsop.

■ "The object of your mission is to explore the Missouri river, & such principal stream of it, as, by its course and communication with the waters of the Pacific Ocean, whether the Columbia, Oregon, Colorado or any other river may offer the most direct & practicable water communication across this continent for the purposes of commerce."

President Thomas Jefferson, July 4, 1803

Fort Clatsop National Memorial commemorates the 1805–6 winter encampment of the thirty-three-member Lewis and Clark Expedition on a 125-acre site near the Pacific Ocean in northwestern Oregon. A reconstructed fort, the historic canoe landing, and a spring interpret the rich original setting of forests and wetlands that sustained the Corps of Discovery for three months before the start of their return journey across North America.

Lewis and Clark's stay in the rain-drenched, flea-infested encampment is recorded in *The Journals of the Expedition Under the Command of Capts. Lewis and Clark.* Arriving on December 7, 1805, Captain William Clark recorded the fort's site about three miles up the Netul River, as marked by a sign on the highland on the Lewis and Clark River's western bank, ". . . [we] formed our camp in a thick grove of lofty pines, about two hundred yards from the water, and thirty feet above the level of high tides." The next day construction started on a fort; by Christmas Eve the expedition was under shelter.

After the outward journey's year-and-a-half of travel, the Corps of Discovery followed the local Indians' advice that plentiful elk along the south side of the river could supply the expedition's need of meat for food and hides for new clothing. Fifteen miles south along the ocean shore, the party established a salt works to boil seawater for much-needed salt for the homeward journey. The one hundred and six days of the winter encampment was spent in preparation for this event. Drenching rainfall plagued the party. Clark noted twelve days free of rain; the sun was observed on only six days.

As members of the party hunted, built canoes, made clothing (four hundred pairs of moccasins for the return trip) or went to the sea to make salt, the captains continued to compile their journals. Captain Lewis collected information, studied, and wrote in detail about the native Indian tribes, flora and fauna, and local animals. Captain Clark wrote about the geography of the region and prepared a master map of the route from his daily running charts and information gleaned from the Indians encountered on the journey from the Mississippi to the Pacific.

DEPARTURE

Despite the hardship of endless rain, tempered by the hospitality of the eponymous Clatsop tribe, Sergeant John Ordway recorded, "The rain ceased and it became fair about Meridian, at which time we loaded our canoes and at 1:00 P.M. left Fort Clatsop on our homeward-bound journey. At this place we had wintered and remained from the 7th of Decr. 1805 to this day and have lived as well as we had any right to expect, and we can say that we were never without 3 meals of some kind a day either of pore Elk meat or roots, notwithstanding the repeated rain which has fallen almost constantly since we passed the long narrows . . . indeed w[e] have had only [blank space in MS] days fair weather since that time."

By the 1850s the only evidence of the expedition's fort was a few foundation logs. Overgrown by second-growth forest and difficult to locate with precision, the Oregon Historical Society resolved late in 1899 to identify the site of Fort Clatsop for the purpose of erecting a monument. Testimony of former residents of the locale provided information on the location and speculation on the layout of a group of separate cabins. The society acquired a three-acre tract in 1901, a marker was placed on the property in 1912, and the citizens of Astoria improved the site.

Discovery of Clark's pocket fieldbooks in 1903 revealed two plans of Fort Clatsop and the vicinity. Etched on the elk-hide cover was a sketch of two parallel cabins, each about fifty feet long and fourteen to sixteen feet wide, containing a total of seven rooms and separated by a parade ground twenty feet wide. A stockade closed one end of the parade ground and the other end was secured by stockade walls and a gate. There were three rooms on the west side of the fifty-foot-square fort for eight or nine men each. Along the opposite side were quarters for Lewis and Clark; the Charbonneau family (Toussaint Charbonneau, a French-Canadian interpreter; his Shoshone wife, Sacagawea; and their infant son); the orderly rooms for the fort's guards; a storeroom for trade goods, meat, and other provisions; and a sentry box outside the door of the storage room to check for spoilage and clearing the fort of Indian guests each night.

The reconstruction, built in 1955 for the occasion of the Lewis and Clark sesquicentennial celebration through the efforts of many citizens of Astoria and Clatsop County, follows the plans and notes of Clark's fieldbooks and information collected by the Oregon Historical Society. A team of skilled Finnish workmen cut and shaped the logs that were then separated for treatment with chemical preservatives and reassembled on the site. Foundation logs and walls laid horizontally and saddle-notched, chinked originally with mud, are cut with uniform projections at intersecting walls. The shed roof, covered with cedar-shake shingles, slopes inward to the parade ground. Stockade walls are pointed-end pallisers; twin log columns support a horizontal log beam at the entrance gate.

The restored fort was dedicated on August 21, 1995. The property was transferred to the federal government and an expanded 125-acre site added to the National Park System on May 29, 1958. Today, the visitor has the opportunity to visit the fort, spring, and canoe landing. From June through Labor Day, members of the park staff in period costumes demonstrate some of the frontier skills used at Fort Clatsop in the winter of 1805–6. About fifteen miles southwest of the forts on the beach at Seaside, Oregon, a memorial site marks the alleged location of the salt works.

2 Captain William Clark's plan of Fort Clatsop and vicinity

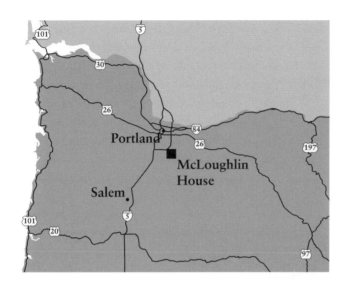

3 McLoughlin House National Historic Site
Oregon City, Clackamas County, Oregon

The house is located in McLoughlin Park at 713 Center Street between Seventh and Eighth Streets. It is about nine blocks east of Interstate 205. Take exit south to McLoughlin Boulevard and turn right on Seventh Street. The house is less than four blocks east of Pacific Highway (U.S. 99).

Remembered for his kind and generous treatment of the American settlers who came to the Oregon Territory, Dr. John McLoughlin lived in this house from 1847 until his death in 1857. The site commemorates the life and accomplishments of a key actor in the settlement and development of the area that was to become the states of Oregon, Washington, Idaho, and parts of Montana, Wyoming, and British Columbia. The .63-acre site was designated a national historic site on June 27, 1941, and renamed on January 16, 1946. The site is an affiliated area with the National Park System and is owned and administered by the McLoughlin Memorial Association.

CHIEF FACTOR—JOHN McLOUGHLIN

Born into a Quebec farming family on October 19, 1784, McLoughlin was nineteen when signed on as physician for the North West Company, where he soon worked his way up to company partner. After the merger with the Hudson's Bay Company in 1821, McLoughlin was sent to the Oregon country to preside over the vast wilderness on which the organi-

3 John McLoughlin

zation pinned its hopes for expansion. As Chief Factor (superintendent of trade), McLoughlin oversaw the construction of the new headquarters at Fort Vancouver, promoted agriculture, opened new trapping routes, and took in an impressive profit.

McLoughlin's imposing size and appearance helped to keep the peace and win respect. He stood six feet four inches tall in a land where most Indians and French Canadians were of short stature. He was heavily boned. A ruddy complexion, massive brows above light blue eyes, and thick blonde hair, combined with a habitually grave expression and a slow dignity in movement, impressed the Indians.

McLoughlin's reign as chief factor meshed with the eventual settlement of the boundary dispute between Britain and the United States. British domination of the region, based on the fur trade, declined with the dwindling fur supply and demand. Immigrant wagon trains poured into the region from the Oregon Trail. The thousands of American farmers clearing farmland would inevitably tip the balance of power. McLoughlin defied company orders to discourage settlement, extending credit for food, seeds, and farm tools to the settlers, then steered them southward into the Willamette Valley. His generosity gained him respect as a paternalistic figure who would never turn away those in need.

Sir George Simpson, Hudson's Bay Company Director of Operations in North America, disapproved of McLoughlin's open-handed treatment of the settlers. In 1845 McLoughlin was forced to resign.

Completed in 1846, the house is a two-story wood-frame structure, elegant in its design of simple proportions and details. Where most Willamette Valley immigrant families lived in crude log cabins, the house was imposing for its size and construction of completely finished lumber—local timber and prefabricated trim shipped from a Boston factory. Built on a foundation of ashlar-laid masonry (tall enough for a root cellar), with double-hung windows in large window openings, horizontal lap siding, and double-pitch roof, the house was a prominent feature in the frontier settlement of Oregon City.

The first floor consisted of a large parlor, a dining room, a reception room, and McLoughlin's office. Upstairs were three bedrooms, as well as a sitting room and hallway that often doubled as a guest room. The kitchens were in separate buildings out back. Today, the house is furnished to resemble its appearance during the McLoughlin occupancy. The dining room table and chairs belonged to the McLoughlins and are the same ones they used at Fort Vancouver. Other furnishings are period pieces that belonged to the McLoughlin family, the Hudson's Bay Company, and early Oregon settlers.

McLoughlin became a U.S. citizen in 1851 to support his property claims, and served as Oregon City mayor that year. Until his death in 1857, he owned two sawmills, a gristmill, a granary, a general store, and a shipping concern. He loaned money for commercial ventures and also donated land for schools and churches.

After the death of his wife, Marguerite, the house was sold, added onto, and for years used as a hotel. In 1903 early preservation efforts were initiated. The work did not begin in earnest until the threat of demolition in 1909 inspired the founding of the McLoughlin Memorial Association. The house was moved to McLoughlin Park, high on a bluff overlooking the town, on land donated by McLoughlin to the city in 1850.

For more information, write to the Curator, McLoughlin House National Historic Site, 613 Center Street, Oregon City OR 97045, or call (503) 656-5146.

4a Oregon Caves Chateau, 1936

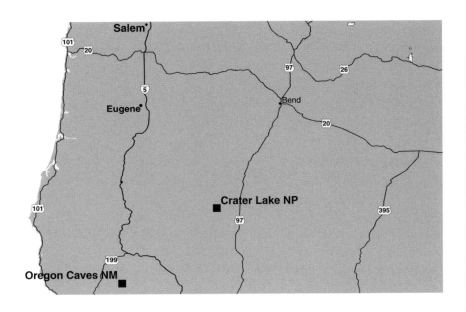

4 Oregon Caves National Monument

Josephine County, Oregon

www.nps.gov/orca

Oregon Caves National Monument is fifty miles south of Grants Pass, Oregon, and seventy-six miles northeast of Crescent City, California, via U.S. 199. It is reached by Oregon Highway 46, an eighteen-mile-long narrow, mountainous highway east of Cave Junction.

■ "The prime significance of Oregon Caves' Chateau lies in the designer's extraordinarily creative use of the limited building site and how he allowed the site to dictate major architectural choices. Inseparable from that is the extremely high integrity of the building, the furnishings, and the site."

**Laura Soullière Harrison, *Architecture in the Parks*,
National Historic Landmark Theme Study**

The Oregon Caves National Monument is small in size but rich in diversity. The 488-acre site protects caves carved out of limestone formations with all of the earth's six main rock types, unusually large bats, virgin forests of Douglas fir, and exceptional rustic architecture in a National Historic

District and the National Historic Landmark Oregon Caves Chateau. The caves are off the well-traveled tourist path in southwestern Oregon's Siskiyou Mountains. The Monument was proclaimed in 1909 and transferred from the Forest Service to the National Park Service in 1933.

In 1874 a twenty-four-year-old Oregonian named Elijah Davidson came upon the caves while deer hunting. During the 1890s, local business interests tried to exploit the area's resort potential. Fortunately the remote location of the caves limited the number of hardy visitors who made their way into the Siskiyou wilderness. A visit in 1907 by Joaquin Miller—the "Poet of the Sierra"—marked the beginning of a concerted effort to promote the caves' protection and preservation. By 1909 lobbying had become so intense that the site was designated a National Monument by President William Howard Taft under the jurisdiction of the Forest Service, U.S. Department of Agriculture.

Disgruntled local businessmen pushed their congressional delegation to have the area changed to a national park. They hoped that a redesignation would ease the federal regulations that made it difficult to build a resort and access road in a Forest Service area. Changes in 1915 to the Forest Service regulations on leased lands for hotel and recreation sites renewed local interest in developing Oregon Caves. In 1922 an automobile road reached the park, and in 1923 a group of businessmen from Grants Pass formed the Oregon Caves Company to manage the concession at the monument. The company planned to offer food services, overnight lodging, and cave tours, and began by building the Chalet, a handful of cottages, and some tent houses.

By 1929 a company spokesman announced plans to construct the Chateau. In 1933 the monument was transferred from the Forest Service to the National Park Service, and the Oregon Caves Chateau was constructed the next year. The original two-story Chalet was expanded in 1941–42 and currently serves as the office for the gift shop and cave. The bottom floor is the original chalet, while the added story now houses employees.

4a Oregon Caves Chateau

4a Oregon Caves Chateau

The Chateau at Oregon Caves National Monument is one of the least-known lodges in the National Park System. Although relatively unrecognized, the Chateau is a tour de force of organic architecture and well worth a visit. This six-story lodge built into a gorge is a strong architectural presence in a rich forest setting among tumbling waterfalls and moss-covered marble ledges.

To obtain a suitable design for the Chateau, the Oregon Caves Company contracted with a Grants Pass architect and builder, Gust Liam. Construction on the Chateau began in 1932 and was completed in 1934 at a cost of $50,000. The challenge for Liam was enormous. The steep sides of the gorge had to accommodate a road and parking area, limiting the available building space. An existing development of Chalet and employee housing with shaggy cedar bark siding, long roof shingles, and steeply pitched roofs set an architectural precedent for the complex.

Rather than perching the Chateau on the mountainside, similar to the other buildings at the Monument, Liam chose to have it span the small gorge and blend agreeably into the site. The cave's stream discharged through the gorge, and the steady waters were used to architectural advantage. Liam allowed a small portion of the stream to pass through the dining room, channeled through a culvert in the Chateau's basement. He physically brought the outside in and reinforced this interplay with enormous picture windows. Visitors could sit in the dining room enjoying a tasty meal while looking out into the thick, green forest, a small stream rippling past their feet.

Liam scaled down the perceived mass of the building by constructing the largest portion inside the gorge. From the "ground" level, where the drive curves around the building, the visitor senses a two-story building—something smaller in scale than the trees in the forest, and something that fits with the terrain and rural atmosphere of the development. The full six-story height can be seen only from a distance across the gorge. Skillfully adapting the floor plan to the site, Liam placed a trapezoidal-plan central wing forty-one feet deep and thirteen feet wide on the entrance side that widens to forty-eight feet facing the gorge. A pair of rectangular wings approximately thirty-five feet wide by sixty feet long extend at angles away from the central wing; the long dimension extends into the gorge. The wings facing the gorge were originally united by a wood veranda at the second, third, and fourth floor, which has since been replaced by metal fire escapes.

Liam adapted other site influences into the Chateau's design. The exterior of the Chateau was covered in shaggy cedar-bark shiplap siding, so the building matched the texture of the surrounding conifer forest. Steeply pitched main gable roofs, pierced by shed-roof dormers and further broken by gabled-roof dormers, all with long shake shingles, maintain a scale compatible with the setting. In spite of its formidable mass, the building does not appear to intrude on its setting.

Most of the construction materials are of local origin. Log timbers of Douglas fir were cut a short distance away and trimmed at a mill on the Caves Highway. The cedar bark for the vertical siding came from a nearby railroad-tie-cutting operation. Marble for the double fireplace in the lobby was blasted out of bedrock on the site.

The Chateau has a wood-frame superstructure on a concrete foundation that rests on natural bedrock. The lowest two floors house mechanical equipment and storage areas. The dining room, coffee shop, and kitchen areas are on the third floor—the same level as the lower trout pool grotto at the immediate head of the gorge. The fourth floor is at road level and

4a Oregon Caves Chateau Lobby

contains the entrance lobby and some guestrooms. The two upper floors have additional guestrooms and the manager's living quarters.

The large lobby on the fourth floor, accessible from the parking lot, contains a double fireplace. Douglas-fir log columns thirty inches in diameter and massive eighteen-by-twenty-four-inch beams felled from surrounding hillsides support the timber framing in the lobby and lounge areas. The subtle pale-gray wood in the room has a history; construction workers beat sacks of cement against the wooden posts to loosen up the bags' contents. Tiny particles of cement became imbedded in the wood. As the building neared completion, the crew stained wood not initially tinted by the cement to match it.

A handsome rustic staircase of oak, madrone, pine, and fir leads downstairs from the lobby to the dining room and upstairs to the guest rooms. Oak treads three inches thick rest on a massive pair of stringers. The darker wood of the peeled madrone balusters and the lighter wood of the handrails and newel posts are smooth-finished but retain softened gnarls and knots. Natural light from the large windows overlooking the trout pool highlights the stairwell and creates a pleasing contrast with the darker lobby.

Construction on the Chateau was underway for a year when the National Monument came under jurisdiction of the National Park Service in 1933. As the federal agency responsible for approving all of the construction

4a Oregon Caves Chateau Lobby

4a Oregon Caves Chateau Bar

in the National Monument, the National Park Service brought its group of experts to the project—the people responsible for developing the rustic design ethic. Additional funding under the Civilian Conservation Corps employed hundreds of young men to build stone retaining walls, two trout pools and a waterfall, a campfire circle, and various walkways.

The development at Oregon Caves was typical of work in other national parks and monuments during the 1930s. The concessioner worked closely with the Plans and Design branch of the National Park Service, headed by landscape architect Thomas C. Vint. Architectural drawings were presented to the National Park Service technical staff for approval and, possibly, suggestions on how the building could better fit into its environment. Simultaneously, National Park Service landscape architects prepared landscape plans to enhance the site. At Oregon Caves, they laid out the stone walls and located sites for reflecting pools. The on-site landscape architect chose rubble boulders at the site, singling out the ones he wanted according to texture, color, and weathering. The resulting stone walls have a natural-looking aged appearance that make the walls blend in with the weathered

4a Oregon Caves Chateau and Chalet, 1936

bedrock exposed around the site. This thoughtful approach to site design further enhances the rustic feeling around the Chateau. The concessioners and National Park Service designers successfully achieved a development in harmony with the site: the hotel, residences, and parking areas fit comfortably into the surrounding landscape.

National Park Service architectural historian Laura Soullière Harrison describes how little the building has changed over time: "Today's visitor is still enchanted by the rustic sense of place that the builder and the landscape architects created. Entering the area is very much like traveling back into the 1930s. Trout still swim in the small pools. Even the smell of the aging fiberboard contributes to that undeniably nostalgic feeling. The Chateau is more weathered but the furnishings are entirely original. More important than these subjective responses to the spaces is the strong architectural presence of the Chateau with its steep roofs and shaggy exterior. The builders' intent to create a structure in harmony with the surrounding landscape, and the landscape architects' enhancement of the setting, remain artistic pieces of the past."

Timberline Lodge

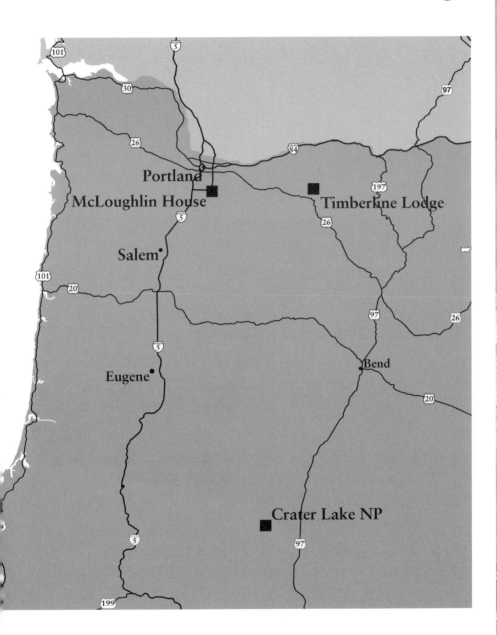

Portland

McLoughlin House

Timberline Lodge

Salem

Eugene

Bend

Crater Lake NP

5 Timberline Lodge (above); detail, main entrance door (facing)

5 Timberline Lodge

Government Camp, Clackamas County, Oregon

www.timberlinelodge.com

Timberline lodge is located in the Mount Hood National Forest about sixty miles east of Portland via Interstate 84. Leave Interstate 84 at exit 16 (Wood Village), turn right at the stop sign onto 242nd, follow 242nd to Burnside (approx. 3 mi.), and turn left on Burnside, which turns into Highway 26 East. Follow Hwy 26 East to the Timberline Road turn-off (about 40 mi.), turn left on the Timberline access road; follow the road to Timberline.

■ "It's not all that much in retrospect. A few hundred thousand dollars. Credit with local contractors was extended way beyond what was reasonable. They knew I was trying to build something, and not take something out of it."

Operator Richard L. Kohnstamm, commenting on negotiating his first lease with the Forest Service for the derelict Timberline Lodge in 1955.

5 Timberline Lodge

Timberline Lodge is a winter resort, a living museum of crafts, and a major achievement of breathtaking design and construction just above the timberline on the south slope of Mount Hood. It is a dramatic, hexagonal-shaped stone-and-timber structure, with steeply pitched roofs and flanking wings—a dazzling piece of architecture. The building's form and materials were designed to withstand the heavy winds and deep snows and to harmonize with the mountain. The volcanic peaks of Mounts Jefferson, Washington, and the Three Sisters are visible a hundred miles to the south. Although an exception in this guidebook as a historic structure not located in a unit of the National Park System, the National Historic Landmark Timberline Lodge is widely regarded as one of the finest 1930s Works Progress Administration designs.

The design is described as "Cascadian"—a grand American version of the European chateau and alpine chalet. The lodge's hexagonal central unit with its dramatic, peaked-head house is flanked by two wings of unequal length. A lofty main lounge built of massive stone and hand-adzed timber extends to a wing with fifty-nine guest rooms to the west, and lounges, dining room, and conference center added in 1975 to the east. The building echoes Mount Hood's majestic silhouette, presenting a form and massing designed to meet the demands of heavy snow and fierce winds.

The silvery gray weathered stone and wood exterior, close in tone to the surrounding natural colors, give the lodge a special dignity. The massive basalt boulders at the ground-floor level meet the steeply sloping shake roof, which extends nearly to the ground in places to protect against heavy snow-falls and spring runoffs. Hand-split cedar roof shakes and board-and-batten siding merge in color with the stone base and chimneys to a warm and invit-ing tone of natural materials. Board and battens are placed two feet apart to conform to the large scale of lodge. The perceived length of the guest room wing is reduced by the use of shingles on part of the east wing balanced by clapboard siding over most of the west wing, including the conference center. Double-hung windows, dormers, and alternating vertical rhythms add to the overall architectural character.

GILBERT STANLEY UNDERWOOD

Designated a depression-era Works Progress Administration project in 1935, the lodge was conceived for Forest Service ownership and private lease management. The Forest Service called upon Gilbert Stanley Underwood to act as consulting architect. Underwood's reputation as a designer for National Park Service projects in Yosemite and for the Union Pacific Railroad in southern Utah brought to the project an experienced hand. Underwood was then working for the federal government in Washington, and his representative, Stanley Stonaker, worked on the proj-ect from a Los Angeles office. Underwood's preliminary sketches were acknowledged as basic to the lodge's eventual form, including his con-cept of a large hexagonal core with guest wings extending outward at angles. Limited funds made it impossible for the Forest Service to hire Underwood as a private architect, so the final drawings for the lodge were prepared by Forest Service staff, and Underwood was consulted by the decorators about the decor.

167

5 Timberline Lodge

When President Franklin Delano Roosevelt dedicated Timberline Lodge on September 28, 1937, work had been under way since June 1936. Building and furnishing the lodge in fifteen months were impressive undertakings. A road was built to connect the site with a worker's camp seven miles away at Summit Meadows. Workers, paid ninety cents an hour, were housed there in tents and trucked daily, summer and winter, to the work site. A contract with the Lorenz Brothers of Portland required that 90 percent of the work crew be Works Progress Administration employees, and crews were switched every two weeks to employ as many people as possible.

Timberline Lodge is a significant expression of the Great Depression, having been built by hundreds of Works Progress Administration workers, with regional design themes and materials used wherever possible. All work was done by hand, utilizing traditional building and craft techniques. Tools were simple, allowing the integrity of the basic material to stand in balance and harmony with its function.

An inspired team effort was necessary to unite the unskilled crew. Speed was essential because survival of the Works Progress Administration was uncertain. Despite the fast-paced construction schedule and harsh weather, there were no major accidents. Men worked as a matter of pride.

Recorded reminiscences of contributors to the project are emotional, articulating their dedication to something special.

Construction pushed ahead through a severe winter, with hardly a day's loss of work. Snowplows routinely opened the access road, and small stoves were set up to warm the stonemasons' hands. Interior finish work continued into a second winter, and the lodge was opened to the public in February 1938. The Works Progress Administration recorded $695,730 for construction costs; with roads and grounds added, the total was more than a million dollars.

The building materials were all local. Giant Douglas fir and pine were turned into rafters and columns, and native oak, pine, and cedar were used for flooring and paneling. More than four hundred tons of stone was quarried nearby and used for exterior stairways, buttresses, and chimneys. Thirty-man teams split cedar into thirty-six-inch shakes for the exterior.

Wherever possible, recycled materials were used. Utility poles were carved into newel posts and medallions, decorated with figures of wild rams, opossum, eagles, pelicans, owls, and bear cubs. Scraps from earlier Works Progress Administration sewing projects found new life in appliquéd bedspreads and curtains. Old railroad tracks were transformed into massive andirons, hinges for doors and gates, window grilles, and a weathervane to crown the head house. Even uniforms and blankets from the Civilian Conservation Corps were cut into strips and hooked into rugs.

5 Timberline Lodge, arch

5 Timberline Lodge, six-sided chimney

5 Timberline Lodge Main Lounge, fireplace

With its stone and timber designed for heavy use by hikers and skiers, the ground-level entrance under the main porch has a grotto-like feeling. The main lounge in the hexagonal-plan head house soars to a web of hand-hewn timber trusses supported by a massive six-sided chimney with large fireplaces. The design of the main lounge shows restraint in furnishings and decoration, allowing the drama of the large space to dominate the room's character. The hexagonal theme is carried throughout the construction and repeated in furnishings. Six great timber columns, each three-and-a-half feet in diameter, support the balconies and roof; they were shaped into hexagonals with broadaxe and foot-adze. The carver, Henry Steiner, agreed to shape them for twenty-five dollars each if the logs were turned at his request as he worked.

A major design element, the graceful Timberline Lodge arch of curved timber posts and lintel arches, is repeated throughout the lodge in doorways and in furniture design, including the hand-carved Douglas-fir backs of the dining room chairs.

The original guest rooms on the first and second floors varied in size and theme. Although twenty-three different schemes were employed, they repeated only two or three times, each carried out in fabrics and rugs, carvings on the furniture, and botanical watercolors. Each room contained hand-crafted beds, dressing tables, loveseats and chairs, and parchment-and-iron floor and table lamps.

Decorative details inside and outside the lodge seem to have been used at the designers' whimsy. Buffalo and bear heads carved on log ends stare from under the eaves, and rams' heads flank the main entrance. A thunderbird wood-carved relief on the lintel over the entrance door was inspired by a design that one of the architects happened upon in his daughter's *Campfire Girls' Handbook.* Old utility poles brought in from Portland for $2.10 apiece were transformed into posts decorated with carved representations of Pacific Northwest birds and animals as well as geometric Native American designs.

5 Timberline Lodge, main entrance door

5 Timberline Lodge Dining Room, entrance

Wrought-iron work adorns the main entrance door and exterior window grilles. The same deft handiwork is carried throughout the interiors, as seen in the andirons wrought from recycled railroad tracks, the door hardware, ashtrays, and furniture, and the elegant gates that frame the dining room entrance. Overall coordination of furnishings and decorations was supervised by Margery Hoffman Smith, a Portland decorator. The project was conceived as an exercise in the Arts & Crafts style: to teach basic handicraft skills and to produce attractive everyday objects of "honest" design. Trial designs by Mrs. Smith and two crafts supervisors, O. B. Dawson and Ray Neufer, were first crafted and then recorded on scale drawings for reproduction in workshops. Located at the construction work site and in Portland, shops for Works Progress Administration workers produced wooden and wrought-iron furniture; handwoven fabric for upholstery, draperies and bedspreads; hand-stitched appliquéd draperies; hooked rugs; wrought-iron gates; and door hardware and straps. A high level of performance was required; anything of shoddy quality was rejected or remade.

Mrs. Smith convinced the Federal Arts Project to commission original works of art for Timberline Lodge. Oil paintings, watercolors, wood reliefs, mosaics, and newel-post carving throughout the lodge were created by artists paid $90 a month. The Timberline collection includes eleven oil canvasses and 144 watercolors of mountain plants. The Blue Ox Bar, an afterthought, is decorated with three glass-mosaic scenes that depict the Paul Bunyan legend. Enriching the lodge, the artwork achieves one of the project's main goals: to serve as a living museum for the people of Oregon.

The lodge was built in perilous times. After it opened, it was available year-round until 1942, when it was closed through the war years. Sadly, the lodge was subject to abuse and theft from the start. The laxity of Forest Service supervision coupled with poor management led to its closing in February 1955 for unpaid electric bills.

A weekend skier, Richard L. Kohnstamm, fell in love with the lodge despite its appearance. He arranged a lease with the Forest Service and set out to restore Timberline to its former brilliance. Years of hard work followed, involving repairs to the heating and water systems and careful restoration of the interiors and furnishings. In 1975 a group called Friends of Timberline organized as a nonprofit foundation to assist in the repairs.

A dedicated management company and the Friends assure a successful future for the lodge. In Kohnstamm's words: "I take care of the plumbing and the Friends take care of the artwork." The Forest Service has recognized this successful partnership by awarding Kohnstamm's company an operating lease to the year 2005. In 1981 the Forest Service built a lodge nearby for day skiers. It is sensitive to Timberline Lodge in design and placement and helps ease the burden of heavy usage at the older structure.

By pooling the funds of the operating company, the Friends of Timberline, and the Forest Service, the life of the lodge will be extended. Franklin D. Roosevelt's prediction—"a place for generations of Americans to come . . . a new adjunct to the national prosperity"—is well on its way to being fulfilled.

2 Mount Rainier National Park

San Juan Island NHP

Olympic NP

Seattle

Olympia

Mount Rainier NP

Fort Vancouver NHS

1 Fort Vancouver National Historic Site, Bastion

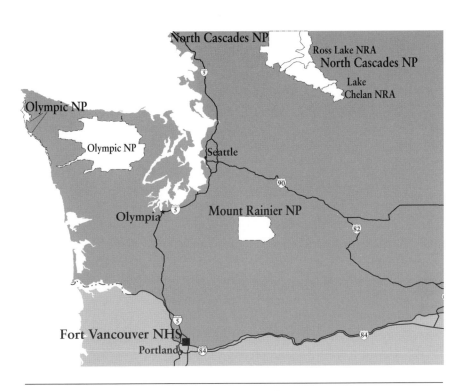

Olympic NP

North Cascades NP

Ross Lake NRA
North Cascades NP

Lake
Chelan NRA

Olympic NP

Seattle

90

Olympia

Mount Rainier NP

82

5

Fort Vancouver NHS

Portland

84

84

1 Fort Vancouver National Historic Site
Vancouver, Clark County, Washington
www.nps.gov/fova

The park is located in the city of Vancouver, Washington. From Interstate 5, exit on Mill Plain Boulevard and drive east on East Evergreen Boulevard following signs to the visitor center. From Interstate 205, exit on Washington Highway 14; go west about 6 miles and take Interstate 5 North, exit on Mill Plain Boulevard and drive east on East Evergreen Boulevard following signs to the visitor center.

■ No events of great drama occurred here. No battles were fought, no armed or diplomatic confrontations, no international treaties were signed in the chief factor's residence. Instead, Fort Vancouver represented, and still represents, long-term stability between two peoples and two governments.

Fort Vancouver, National Park Service Handbook

Surrounded by twentieth-century sights and sounds, Fort Vancouver National Historic Site is the reconstruction of a Hudson's Bay Company trading post. It recalls a time when the fort on the north bank of the Columbia River was a frontier place where top-hatted factors and clerks once mingled with voyageurs and Indians. For thirty-five years—a brief passage in the history of the Pacific Northwest—this remote trading post was the focus of a political and economic struggle for regional dominance.

From 1825 to 1849 Fort Vancouver was the western headquarters of the Hudson's Bay Company's fur trading operations. Under the leadership of John McLoughlin, the fort became the center of political, cultural, commercial, and manufacturing activities in the Pacific Northwest. Despite its military appearance, employees and settlers feared little from an attack. The enclosing palisade walls were for security purposes, primarily as a deterrent to theft. The cannons were never fired in anger, only to salute approaching ships.

Fort Vancouver offers a step back in time; try to ignore the intrusive interstate highway bridge from Portland across the Columbia River, the high-powered transmission lines, and the light aircraft from an adjacent airport, and let this re-created British outpost bring to life the era of Northwest trappers and traders. The National Park Service has meticulously crafted a journey for visitors that begins with an interpretive center and leads back into history. Inside the fifteen-foot-tall Douglas fir pickets surrounding a grassy rectangle (734 by 318 feet), period-furnished structures and reenactments by people in costumes of the time instill the visitor with a sense of the fort's history.

One visitor commented that the best time to see Fort Vancouver is "on a foggy weekend morning when the sights and sounds of this century are muted and all you can see are the tall fir timbers of the palisade and the outline of its buildings inside." Then modern intrusions are erased and the scene returns to the timeless quality of the palisade, the river plain, and the Columbia River flowing westward to the Pacific.

Struggle for an Empire

The American Northwest in the late 1700s and early 1800s was a vast expanse of land that stretched from Russian Alaska south to Spanish California, and from the Pacific Ocean east to the Rocky Mountains. It was rich fur-trapping and -trading country, and Americans, British,

Spanish, and Russians vied for control of the Pacific coast and Columbia River watershed.

Successive discoveries brought the region under conflicting claims. Within weeks of each other in 1792, the American Robert Gray and British George Vancouver "discovered" the mouth of the Columbia River. Fur traders and other commercial interests valued the Columbia River as a means of reaching the continent's interior. The river system drains into much of the Northwest and provided access to some of the richest fur-trapping country in North America.

The Louisiana Purchase (1803) secured a claim on the Oregon Country for the United States, and Lewis and Clark's expedition reports proclaimed the rich resources of the region. In the War of 1812, conflicting British and American claims boiled over into the Pacific Northwest, and the British seized the town of Astoria on the south bank at the mouth of the Columbia River. The United States argued for possession of territory south of the forty-ninth parallel; the British insisted that the border should follow the Columbia River from where it crosses the forty-ninth parallel to the ocean. A Convention of Joint Occupancy in 1818 provided both nations with equal trade and settlement rights for the next decade, when the situation would again be reviewed.

Astoria (then Fort George), on the Columbia estuary, provided temporary headquarters for the British North West Company and its 1821 successor, the Hudson's Bay Company. They abandoned the fort in favor of a new north-bank location one hundred miles upstream—one that would both strengthen British claims between the Columbia River and the forty-ninth parallel and act as a political and economic center for the Hudson's Bay Company.

A north-bank site was located just above the Willamette River. An important feature of the location was that oceangoing vessels of up to two hundred tons could ascend without lightening their loads. The site for Fort Vancouver was on a bluff of open land three miles wide and a mile deep. The river floodplain and rich soil above it could support orchards and gardens. The bluff was long and broad and offered good protection against surprise attack via either water or land. Hauling supplies from the water's edge was a minor inconvenience compared to the secure defensive position. Construction progressed slowly, as merchandise had to be transferred from Fort George.

When the Convention of Joint Occupancy was renewed in 1828, it increased the need to reinforce the position of the British and the Hudson's Bay Company. Pressured by the company, Great Britain had refused to accept a United States proposal of the forty-ninth parallel as the boundary. The Americans, equally stubborn, refused to accept the Columbia River as the boundary. A decision was reached to expand Fort Vancouver as the Hudson's Bay Company's principal supply depot and administrative center on the west coast of North America. Additional warehouses, offices, staff quarters, farm buildings, and fields were called for, so the original fort on top of the bluff was abandoned for a new complex nearer the river and its docks, about a half mile to the west and a quarter mile from the riverbank.

Work at a new site began in 1829. A palisade enclosed a dozen buildings—dwellings, warehouses, and workshops—arranged around an interior court. Indians went there to trade, trappers and traders took their furs and departed with goods from the Indians, clerks bustled in and out of the warehouses, and visiting sailors idled between trips. John McLoughlin held the position as chief factor, directing the Hudson's Bay Company Northwest Department, which encompassed an area larger than New England. McLoughlin was six feet four inches tall, and his commanding presence no doubt served him well as he directed construction of the effort. His good relations with the American settlers earned him recognition as "Father of Oregon."

OREGON FEVER

The "Oregon Fever" that swept the United States in the 1840s changed the political future of the American Northwest. Prior to 1840, the only permanent settlers from the East in the region were mostly missionaries serving the Indians or trappers. But in 1841 farmers attracted by the fertile Willamette Valley began to trickle into the area. By 1843 the Great Migration had begun, and wagon trains and herds of livestock were heading for Oregon Territory. Each year the number of migrants increased, and by 1846, when a wagon road was completed over the Cascade Mountains, the non-Indian population in Oregon was close to six thousand. The settlers, who declared possession of the region, established a provisional government in 1843. Accepting the authority of the provisional government brought an end to Fort Vancouver's importance to Hudson's Bay Company.

In June 1846 the United States and Great Britain signed a treaty establishing the forty-ninth parallel as the boundary between the crest of the Rockies and the Strait of Juan de Fuca. The Hudson's Bay Company sold its holdings south of the forty-ninth parallel. In 1848 Congress established the Oregon Territory, and in May 1849 a U.S. military installation, Columbia Barracks, was founded on the bluff overlooking Fort Vancouver's palisade walls.

The remains of the abandoned fort, surrounded by the military reservation, burned to the ground in 1866. Settlement of the Hudson's Bay Company claims in 1869 included the surrender of the post to the United States. Within a few years, Columbia Barracks and cropland covered the twelve hundred acres of Fort Vancouver. Construction of drainage ditches and occasional artillery practice obliterated the last traces of the old buildings and palisade foundations.

1a Preservation and Reconstruction

An act of Congress on June 19, 1948, established Fort Vancouver National Monument. Archaeological work and research followed, and on June 30, 1961, Fort Vancouver National Monument was redesignated as Fort Vancouver National Historic Site. Work proceeded on reconstruction of the original palisade, and by 1966 the north and east walls were completed. Construction on the remainder of the Palisade and Bastion resumed in 1972, and reconstruction began on buildings within the Palisade. The park has an ongoing archaelogical program to support research on the Hudson's Bay Company as well as additional reconstructions. The collection produced by this archaelogical work includes one million items. The collections may be viewed on-site or through the park's Website.

When reconstruction began in 1966, all aboveground traces of the original fort complex had vanished. Archaeological excavation and meticulous research into the fort's recorded history revealed the location and features of the Palisade and buildings now in place. Letters and journals from the fort's earliest visitors provided descriptions, plans, and sketches of the buildings as they evolved over thirty-five years. Invaluable information was

1a Fort Vancouver Kitchen

gleaned from photographs taken during the fort's final years. For some of
the buildings, only informed guesses guided decisions about building design,
interior layouts, and furnishings.

Framing methods used throughout the reconstruction were in the
company's typical French-Canadian post-on-sill style. Sills sixteen by sixteen inches were hewn from logs and laid on the ground or placed on log
posts set on the ground. Grooved uprights at intervals of about six feet
were then mortised into the sills. Walls between the uprights were squared
logs, either adzed or sawn with a tenon on each end, and laid upon the sills
with the tenons in the grooves of the uprights. Large horizontal log headers

1a Fort Vancouver Blacksmith Shop

mortised and tenoned to the uprights ran around the tops of the walls. Additional headroom for a second story, loft, or attic was gained by extend-ing the walls for several feet above the ceiling timber level. Floors and ceiling joists were made of squared timbers notched into sills and header beams. The roofs were formed by rafters and braces dovetailed and pegged for additional strength. Windows and doorframes were formed by uprights tenoned into sills, headers, or horizontal logs. Ceiling beams were mortised into timbers of the course immediately above the window and door headers.

A walk down the rolling surface of the bluff, from the interpretive center past the orchard and garden outside the Palisade, provides a gradual transition into the atmosphere of the mid-nineteenth century. Entry through the massive wooden gates on the north leads visitors onto the grassy plain of the parallelogram-shaped enclosure. The fifteen-foot-high Palisade walls, running 734 feet in one direction and 318 feet across the ends, deceive the eye; the scope here is that of five football fields placed side by side.

1a Fort Vancouver Entrance Gates

PALISADE AND BASTION

The protective walls of Douglas fir logs that enclose Fort Vancouver stand today as they did to receive the western migration to the Oregon Territory in 1845. Douglas fir was used because of its availability. Although it was resistant to rot in the wet climate, replacements were needed every four or five years.

The Palisade's perimeter wall was enlarged at least five times to meet increases in trading activity and business, and at the peak of activity in the 1830s and 1840s measured more than two thousand feet long. Logs of appropriate length were cut off square at the bottom and charred for extra protection. Fifteen feet was a typical height for the pointed or wedge-shaped logs, each five to ten inches in diameter. The logs were placed at a slight tilt toward the interior and were strengthened by horizontal girths of logs mortised and pegged into the posts two to four feet above the ground and below the tops of the pickets. The entrance gates in the fifteen-foot high northwest and southwest Palisade walls were built of Douglas fir. Two leaves opening inward were constructed of three-inch planking placed vertically on the outer face and horizontally on the inner face. A postern door is in one leaf of the gate.

1a Fort Vancouver Palisade and Bastion

1a Fort Vancouver Gun Mounts

The three-story octagonal Bastion at the Palisade's northwest corner was built in the winter of 1844–45 at the height of fears of an American attack on the fort. The first two stories of the post-on-sill bastion were twenty feet square and about twenty feet high. Horizontal rifle loopholes were cut in the twelve-inch-thick log walls. The top floor was octagonal and extended over the base, giving defenders a clear view of the land and a perfect platform from which to protect the fort. Hinged shutters covered three-pound guns mounted on sea carriages and armed for service.

CHIEF FACTOR'S RESIDENCE

The large white house inside Fort Vancouver's palisade walls served as the official residence provided by the Hudson's Bay Company for its chief factor, John McLoughlin. (For further information on John McLoughlin, see Section 2: Oregon, page 152.) As the center of business, social, and political activity for much of the Oregon Country, the house was intended to impress the Indians and settlers with the power and majesty of the London-based company. Construction began in 1829 and took seven years to complete.

When the original Chief Factor's Residence was completed, it was

1a Fort Vancouver Chief Factor's Residence

reputed to be the grandest house north of San Francisco and west of St. Joseph, Missouri. The big house had white clapboard walls and sweeping paired entrance staircases, which greatly impressed visitors. The floor plan in the reconstruction is the result of archaeological research, examination of archives. The building measures approximately eighty by forty feet, is one story high, and contains ten rooms. The main floor was raised about five feet above ground to leave room for a wine cellar below. Curved iron arbors and veranda uprights supported grapevines, which acted as awnings against the sun. A pair of mounted cannons ceremonially guard the entrance.

English values and the rigid class structure of the mother country were perpetuated in the activities of the chief factor's house. Dinners in the twenty-by-thirty-foot common dining room were limited strictly to the company's commissioned officers. Guests to the post were well received, but officers' wives were not welcome. Apprentice clerks were the lowest on the social ladder, only occasionally attending dances at the house. When church services were held in the mess hall, anyone could attend, but this was the only time when common laborers could enter the house.

Some of the comforts of home were brought by ship from England around Cape Horn and up the west coast to the Columbia River. Excavations have yielded shards of export china, earthenware, and other artifacts that provided valuable clues as to what the original furnishings in the house were. A visitor in 1841 described the "elegant Queen's ware" and the "glittering glasses and decanters" that graced the table in the mess hall. The restoration relied heavily upon such written records. Journals and letters that made reference to the Big House have helped restorers know that the original house had pine-boarded walls and ceilings and a Carron stove from Scotland. A copy of von Humboldt's *Personal Narrative of Travels to South America* rests on the chief factor's desk today because a visitor in 1833 wrote about borrowing it from Dr. McLoughlin.

KITCHEN/LAUNDRY

The Kitchen, a building of post-on-sill framing, was directly to the north of the Chief Factor's House and connected to it by a covered passageway. Reconstructed as an 1845 kitchen containing a cooking area, pantry, and larder, as well as living quarters for some of the kitchen staff, it was the scene for the preparation of the main meal of the day, served at midday, for the fifteen or twenty commissioned officers.

A staff of women worked in the laundry room, where they cleaned and pressed the clothing of the chief factor, his family, and the commissioned officers and clerks. A stove heated water, and indoor drying was practiced, following rules of the fort that forbade hanging the laundry out to dry in the yard.

WASHHOUSE

The Washhouse appears on several maps of Fort Vancouver drawn in the 1840s. Very little is known of its appearance or use. The building was probably destroyed by fire in 1852. The reconstruction is based on use as a washing place for clothes, persons, or both.

BAKEHOUSE

The gabled, $1\frac{1}{2}$-story Bakehouse, about twenty-five by forty feet, contained two large brick ovens, with a sleeping loft above for the bakers. The hearth and chimneys in the bakery were located outside the palisade walls as a precaution against fire spreading to other buildings inside the walls.

Several bakers toiled long hours to bake bread for the two hundred to three hundred people at the fort, in addition to the sea biscuit (hardtack) for

1a Fort Vancouver Washhouse

crews of company vessels, traders, and for other forts on the Northwest coast. Dough was mixed in large wooden bins and worked or shaped on long wooden tables. Fires were built directly in the ovens, and after two or three hours the coals were raked out and dough was put in to bake on the hot bricks.

BLACKSMITH SHOP

The Blacksmith Shop served as the principal smithy for the post. Approximately forty-five by twenty-seven feet and post-on-sill framed to the eight-foot-high eaves line, the structure was built directly on the ground and had a hard-packed dirt floor.

The four forges of the Blacksmith Shop produced a variety of items for trade, including ironwork for building and ship repairs. Beaver traps, nails, hardware, parts for gun repair, and the axes coveted by Indians (up to fifty a day) came from the shop's anvils. Iron and steel were imported from England, but fuel to fire the forge was a vexing problem. Coal from England was preferred by the chief factor, but the company's officers resented shipping expensive and bulky coal instead of valuable trading

1a Fort Vancouver Indian Trade Shop and Dispensary

goods. Local coal was of poor quality, and after failed attempts by a
Russian from Sitka to make charcoal from timber, the company relented
and importation of coal resumed.

INDIAN TRADE SHOP AND DISPENSARY

In keeping with the general Hudson's Bay Company practice, the
Indian Trade Shop at Fort Vancouver was under the immediate charge of the
post's surgeon, at least when one was in residence. The building housed not
only the fur trading operations but also the dispensary, doctor's office, and
doctor's residence, and served as the dispensing point for the servants' and
laborers' rations.

The building is eighty by thirty feet, equally divided between the trade
shop and dispensary. Post-on-sill framing reaches twelve feet to the eaves
and ridge roof. Walls are lined with planking, and the ceilings are planked
above the dispensary. In the trade store, ceiling beams and loft planking
are exposed.

The well-stocked shelves and the goods hanging from the ceiling in the
reconstruction represent a typical inventory of trade items available from
Outfit 1845. Caps, hats, clocks, crinolines, powder horns, blankets, kettles,
beaver traps, beads, muskets, and other items were all available for sale or
trade to Indians, settlers, or fort personnel. In 1845 almost twelve hundred

beaver pelts passed across the shop counter, as well as skins from otter, muskrat, mink, fox, wolves, and others—including two grizzly bears.

Fur Warehouse

The animal pelts, primarily beaver, were brought to the fort and kept in warehouses. The furs were pressed into bales before shipping to England. The reconstructed warehouse is one of several originally located within the fort's palisade. On the east side of the building, the visitor can also see the archaeological research and curatorial work that supports collections that are stored on the warehouse's upper floor.

Carpenter Shop

Three to four carpenters and several apprentices were employed at the fort's Carpenter Shop. They also produced window frames and sashes, doors, furniture, carts, wagons, and wooden parts for the tools.

Jail

Dedicated on June 23, 2001, making it the fort's most recent addition, the Jail was originally built between 1841 and 1842.

Mount Rainier

2e
2c
2e
2b
2a
706

Mount Rainier National Park

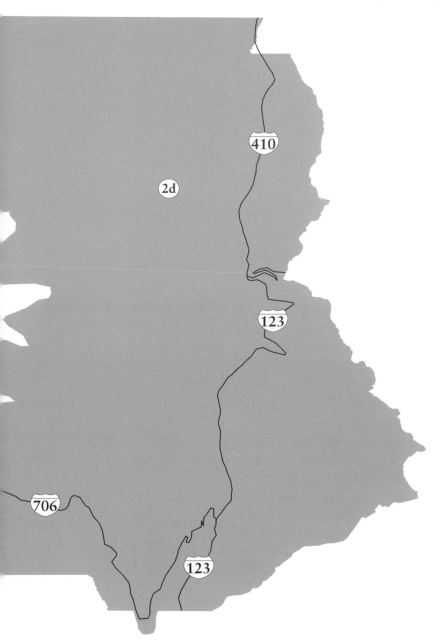

410

2d

123

706

123

2d Mount Rainier National Park, Sunrise Lodge, 1940

2 Mount Rainier National Park
Lewis and Pierce Counties, Washington
www.nps.gov/mora

Mount Rainier National Park is located in west central Washington within an easy drive from Seattle (95 miles), Tacoma (70 miles), and Yakima (103 miles) via Interstate 5. A major road system runs from the southwest entrance (Nisqually) through the southern and eastern parts of the park, with a spur to Sunrise on the northeast side of the mountain. A separate road leads into the Carbon River area in the northwest. The Nisqually entrance is open year-round; eastern mountain passes are closed in the winter. Park headquarters in Ashford is ten miles west of the Nisqually entrance, or take Washington Highways 7 and 706 to the Nisqually entrance; take Highways 410 and 165 to the Carbon River entrance; Highway 410 gives access to the White River and Stevens Canyon entrances; from the south, take U.S. Highway 12 and Washington Highway 123 to the Stevens Canyon entrance.

■ "Of all the fire-mountains, which, like beacons, once blazed along the Pacific Coast, Mount Rainier is the noblest in form. . . . Its massive dome rises out of its forests . . . the loveliest flowers . . . so closely planted and luxuriant that it seems as if Nature, glad to make an open space between woods so dense and ice so deep, were economizing the precious ground, and trying to see how many of her darlings he can get together in one mountain wreath."

John Muir, *Our National Parks*

Seen from a hundred miles away, snow-capped Mount Rainier floats ethereally in the distance. The peak of the truncated volcanic cone in northwestern Washington State rises in dramatic isolation eight thousand feet higher than the surrounding foothills. Seen from above, alternating ridges of rock (called "cleavers") and ice radiate out from the peak to the lowlands. The dense snowpack forms a dozen major glaciers at the seven-thousand-foot level—the largest mass of easily accessible glaciers in the lower forty-eight states. Below the ice fields lies a succession of plant zones to be explored by road or trail. Subalpine meadows are brightened in spring by blossoms that advance behind the melting snow in a stunning array of blue, red, white, pink, and yellow. Dense forests of Alaskan cedar, Douglas fir, western white pine, and western hemlock splay out along the ridges, girdling the peak in thick stands above the lushly shaded forest floor.

The mountain attracted its first formal exploratory expedition in August 1833. William Tolmie, a Hudson's Bay Company employee at nearby Fort Nisqually, organized an expedition to the mountain to collect plants and explore the countryside. Later ascents of the mountain were claimed in the 1850s, but the first well-documented summit climb was undertaken in 1870 by Hazard Stevens and Philemon Trump. Their guide was James Longmire.

JAMES LONGMIRE

James and Vrinda Longmire traveled west with their four children on the Oregon Trail in 1853. He farmed in the Puget Sound area and became a guide for explorers on the mountain. In 1883 Longmire opened a trail and built a cabin for hikers and climbers near the springs that now bear his name. John Muir records renting horses from Longmire and visiting the cabin in 1888. "Longmire Medical Springs" was advertised to travelers, and an enclave of cabins and tents evolved into a bustling community. The site of the Longmire Springs Hotel near Soda Spring, built in 1890 and dismantled and burned by the National Park Service in 1920, ended the Longmires' era of hospitality in the park. The oldest extant historic structure in Mount Rainier National Park is the cabin built in 1888 or 1889 by Elcaine Longmire, James's son. Longmire Springs became the administrative center of the new national park in 1899.

Federal protection of Mount Rainier began in 1893 with the creation of the thirty-five-square-mile Pacific Forest Reserve and expanded in 1897 to an enlarged and renamed Mount Rainier Forest Reserve. After a brief five-year period of lobbying by scientific and conservation groups, including the National Geographic Society, the act establishing Mount Rainier as the nation's fifth national park was signed by President McKinley in 1899. Creation of the park seems to have followed an uncontested assessment of it as worthless. There was not much in the area to attract commercial interests, it was inaccessible, much of the area was bare rock, and there were no valuable minerals. John Ise in *Our National Park Policy* described it as best fitted for "a national park and not much else."

Today, many travelers visit the 235,000-acre Mount Rainier National Park each year to hike, climb, fish, ride trails, and take in the glorious scenery. The park also has a superb collection of historic structures incorporated into a National Historic Landmark designated as the finest example of

2 Camp Muir Shelter

National Park Service master planning in the between-the-wars years. Inaccessibility discouraged settlement, and the early date of the park's founding limited inholding claims or commercial activity to a few visitor accommodations. The buildings at Mount Rainier National Park represent public and private efforts to promote, develop, manage, and protect the park's natural and recreational resources. In their natural settings, the collection of rustic-style structures is one of the most intact and extensive examples of the National Park Service master-planning process. The buildings at the four historic districts—Nisqually, Longmire, Paradise, and Sunrise—along with patrol cabins and bridges, present an appealing and consistent array of rustic park architecture. Together, they exemplify the National Park experience of buildings and landscape designed in harmony with the environment.

As one of the "crown jewels" in the National Park System, Mount Rainier National Park received significant attention in the form of funding allotments and design services that coincided with the emergence of the National Park Service rustic style in the 1920s and 1930s. Park master planning, initiated by the National Park Service in the late 1920s, represents the first fully developed example of the National Park Service master-

2 Mission 66 Visitor Center

planning process. Fortunately, earlier private commercial and federal buildings were of a rustic nature compatible with National Park Service philosophy. Park administration buildings, visitor service centers, residences, and maintenance facilities were all designed and constructed within the framework of the rustic style; the level of detailing was directly proportional to the importance and visibility of the structure. With the exception of Mission 66 influence, with the intrusive, contemporary-designed Visitor Center at Paradise, the park retains the remarkably consistent theme of the historic architecture—buildings, roads, trails, and bridges. The National Park Service Master Plan for post–World War II expansion placed administration and residential structures outside the park at Ashford, west of the Nisqually entrance.

2a Nisqually Entrance

ENTRANCE GATE

A two-hour drive from Seattle to Ashford leads to a sequence of four historic districts beginning at the Nisqually Entrance Gate. A massive log archway spanning the road is the visitor's first contact with rustic architecture. To the right of the entranceway is the finely crafted Oscar Brown Cabin. Early access to Mount Rainier National Park was along a wagon trail from the Nisqually entrance to Longmire Springs. A road built by the U.S. Department of the Interior increased demand for opening the park to automobiles, which occurred in 1907. Entry fees and access by permit justified the funding of this, the park's first government building.

The monumentally proportioned Nisqually Entrance Gate resulted from a visit to the park in 1910 by Secretary of the Interior Richard A. Ballinger, who requested construction of a rustic gateway. Four cedar-log columns almost four feet in diameter and three log beams spanning the roadway were erected in 1911 to create a pergola with a clearance of eighteen feet. The structure was completed in time for President Taft's visit to the park that fall. The massive coped logs stood until they deteriorated and were replaced in 1973. The replacement was identical to the original, including the traditional log sign with the park's name.

2a Oscar Brown Cabin

OSCAR BROWN CABIN

Named in 1906 for the first permanent ranger assigned to the park—Oscar Brown—the cabin was completed in 1908 and served as park headquarters until 1915. The decorative fan of thin logs on a gracefully arched log beam is a unique decorative element of the cabin. The sixteen-by-twenty-two-foot log frame, with projecting saddle-notched corners and a steeply pitched cedar-shingle roof, is a forerunner of the National Park Service rustic style. The interior has plank floors and exposed log walls and ceiling joists. The upper floor, which served as a bedroom, was accessible by ladder. In 1980 the interiors were completely remodeled, additions removed, and the balcony railing was added. The building is presently used as a private residence and is off-limits to the public.

ENTRANCE CHECKING STATION

Just beyond Oscar Brown's cabin is the Entrance Checking Station. Of historical note as one of the earliest projects from the National Park Service Landscape Engineering Division, this log-framed building was completed in 1926 to handle increased park traffic and provide additional ranger quarters. The original design was L-shaped, a plan with carefully proportioned log walls, columns, projecting purlins and joists, and a shake roof with a pole-capped ridge. *Park and Recreation Structures* (1938) critically assessed the design, stating, "A splendid log structure deserving of the impressive background it enjoys. Only the trivial chimneys fail to register to the high standards all other details maintain."

The building's original fine detailing and form has been altered over the years. Interior remodeling, extensions to the porte cochere, and the addition of an entrance-door canopy by the Civilian Conservation Corps in 1936–37 were well-intentioned maintenance work, functional changes made to accommodate traffic and higher vehicles. Unfortunately, the work included removal of a bay from the porte cochere and the addition of an extension without projecting beam ends, thereby creating an imbalance to the keen eye.

2b Longmire Historic District

The road from Nisqually to Paradise offers views of thick forests, rushing streams, and flower borders. One is tempted to bypass the cluster of buildings at Longmire, six miles from the entrance, to reach the Visitor Center at Paradise. What may appear to be a random collection of buildings, made of logs and shingles painted brown, is actually the Longmire Historic District, a group of National Park Service and concessioner structures significant in the interpretive history of Mount Rainier National Park. The administration building, community building, and gas station are National Historic Landmarks.

The horse "trains" run by the Longmires on the road they built between Ashford and the mineral springs reached a favorite destination at the wildflower-carpeted meadow and natural springs. A health-spa resort with a thirty-room hotel, cabins, tents, and bathhouses over the springs attracted visitors and played an important role in developing the land as a national park.

The open meadow on the north side of the road offers a pleasant walk along the Trail of Shadows, bordered by towering Douglas fir and western hemlock, past the remnants of James Longmire's early mineral spring development. Soda Springs, Iron Mike Springs, and Elcaine Longmire's cabin are evidence of what was a bustling community at the turn of the century. The

2b Longmire Cabin

Civilian Conservation Corps replaced the original one-story rectangular cabin in 1934.

LONGMIRE HIKER'S CENTER

Activity at the park intensified when the Tacoma and Eastern Railroad built their National Park Inn. The three-story hotel, which could sleep sixty guests, was completed in 1906, but fire destroyed it twenty years later. In 1911 the railroad expanded its facilities by erecting a clubhouse for guests. Now used as the Longmire Hiker's Center, the building is a well-conceived and well-constructed example of the early rustic design common at Rainier. Form and massing are residential in scale, and Douglas fir logs are used throughout for framing and exterior walls. Logs with plaster-chinked joints and corner saddle notching form the exterior walls. Gable ends are covered by vertical logs at half the diameter of the wall logs and finished with rounded bottoms that create a scalloped shadow on the wall. The shallow-pitched cedar-shingle roof, extended over the front entrance to create a porch, provides a welcoming atmosphere for backcountry hikers. Interior log columns rise to the exposed log-purlin roof framing and act as the center posts for log trusses supporting the roof. The coped-log interior framing is a fine example of rustic-inspired construction.

2b Longmire Hiker's Center

A competitor to James Longmire and the railroad, the Rainier National Park Company entered the area in 1916 with the purchase of the Longmire Springs Hotel and construction of the Paradise Inn between 1916 and 1918. In 1920 the company moved the hotel next to the original National Park Inn on the south side of Longmire Plaza, and it became known as the National Park Inn Annex. After the inn was destroyed by fire in 1926, the Annex was remodeled and assumed the name National Park Inn. The modest appearance of the building—only two and a half stories high with seventeen guest rooms—is explained by its varied history. Never conceived as a dramatic attraction, the unpretentious exterior design and plain interiors were intended simply to provide adequate lodging in a superb setting. Its location, at the start of the ninety-three-mile Wonderland Trail encircling Mount Rainier, and its place of honor as the surviving hotel add to its interest. The inn was renovated in the 1990s.

As visitor activity increased, the park's administration center was shifted from Longmire to Tahoma Woods after World War II. Two early administration buildings are now used as the Library (1910) and the Museum and Visitor Center (1916). The Library originally served as a community kitchen, and the Museum was the park's first Administration Building. Both buildings are log framed, rectangular, and sheltered by steeply pitched cedar-shake roofs.

NISQUALLY SUSPENSION BRIDGE

In 1924 an automobile campground was opened across the Nisqually River from Longmire Springs and the administrative area. A light narrow suspension bridge was replaced with a dramatic log, timber, and plank bridge capable of carrying automobile traffic to and from the campground. Rebuilt in 1951 and 1952, the original log towers were replaced with new towers of heavy sawn posts and milled timbers, and a modified Howe truss replaced the lattice stiffening post. Original wire-rope cables, cable saddles, and steel cable suspenders were reused in the new structure. The fifteen-foot-wide plank-decking roadway is laid on a system of three-by-twelve-inch floor stringers carried by ten-by-eighteen-inch timber floor beams. The present bridge spans 180 feet from center to center of the towers.

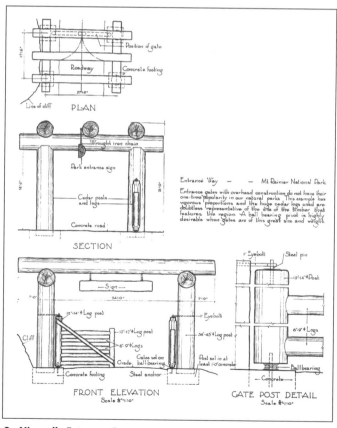

2a Nisqually Entrance Gate

2b Nisqually Suspension Bridge, original structure

A competent and energetic Landscape Engineering Division in the National Park Service's San Francisco office had a strong impact on Longmire. Under the direction of chief architect Thomas C. Vint, a group of talented young men sought out design elements that would make the park buildings compatible with principles of unobtrusive construction in natural settings. Designers and on-site construction supervisors carefully studied the natural materials of the surrounding landscape—scale, color, massing, and texture—and incorporated what they could into their designs. The staff's field experience and mature design skills produced a group of coordinated structures at Longmire that harmonized with the rugged slopes of Mount Rainier. The National Park Service buildings simultaneously acknowledged and emphasized the beauty of the surrounding landscape, using simple sheltering forms and native materials in proper scale.

The general development plan, prepared in 1927 and carried out over the next decade, gave a sense of order to the half-dozen government and

2b Nisqually Suspension Bridge, reconstructed

concessioner buildings south of Longmire Plaza and created a park headquarters with visitor facilities, administrative offices, ranger residences, and maintenance buildings. Three buildings that demonstrate the outstanding talents and efforts of the National Park Service staff are the community building, administration building, and service station.

LONGMIRE COMMUNITY BUILDING

The first of the National Park Service designs was the Longmire Community Building, completed in 1927 at a cost of three thousand dollars. Sited between the suspension bridge and the campgrounds, the two-story, T-plan, timber-framed structure serves as the social and cultural center for Longmire. The approximately thirty-two-by-sixty-one-foot community room has a porch with a shed roof supported on whole log columns sheltering the entrance. The two-story rear wing contains auxiliary spaces to the community room and an apartment on each floor. A semi-octagonal bay window extends from the southwest gable end. Foundation walls of glacial boulders support paired split-log columns with infill walls of thick log veneer on the interior and exterior. A steeply pitched cedar-shingle roof is supported on whole log rafters. The community room front elevation is divided into four

2b Longmire Community Building; detail (p. 195)

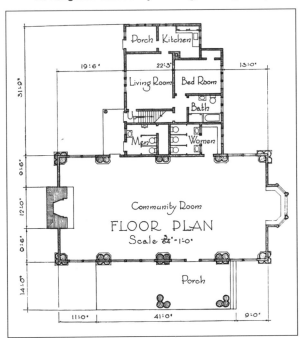

bays with paired casement windows in groups of twos or threes with transoms above. The exterior building form is dominated by the steep roof and rhythms of paired-log columns scaled smaller than the surrounding towering trees.

The interior of the main hall is a revelation of timber columns and trusses, log-slab siding, wooden floor, and cedar tongue-and-groove ceiling planking—all immersed in light from the ribbons of casement and dormer windows. The exterior paired-log column theme is repeated inside in the structural supports for the exposed-log scissor trusses that rise thirty feet above the floor at their peak. Wrought-iron chandeliers and wall sconces add to the character. One gable end wall contains a massive stone fireplace and chimney. Stones in the lower portion are coursed and roughly squared; those above, including the central niche into the chimney, are glacial boulders. The opposite end of the main hall contains a small stage set into a projecting window bay.

The designers' dexterity in manipulating natural materials for both decorative and structural use is illustrated by the paired-log column motif. The porch supports, clusters of three full logs, can be read as a pair from front or side. Log columns on the exterior walls are really half logs reflecting the framing concept and rhythms. Interior pairs of freestanding logs are whole logs used as a framing system independent of the exterior walls to support truss framing. Rather than using the notched corner-log technique of a conventional cabin, the designers created a more formal expression by placing pairs of columns at the corners and using the paired columns to define the bays in the front elevation. The careful workmanship in the coping of exterior and interior logs makes the Community Building a prime example of the rustic style.

Despite these fine touches, *Park and Recreation Structures* described the Community Building as "a park structure of importance that, after pointing the way for many later buildings, has been surpassed in achievement of the subtleties of design and execution that make for true park structural character." Singled out for criticism was the thin roof shingles, the character of the masonry chimneys, and the "almost mechanical stiffness" of the projecting log-purlin rafters with sawn rather than whittled ends. Nevertheless, the building represents an architectural achievement that has been widely popular with National Park Service employees and visitors.

Longmire Administration Building

The most architecturally important National Park Service structure at Longmire is the Administration Building, completed in 1928. Borrowing design features from the 1924 Yosemite Administration Building, the materials used, such as heavy masonry on the first floor and the timber framing on the second story, give this structure its special relationship to the Mount Rainier area. Here, the architects and on-site construction supervisors carefully studied local materials and sensitively incorporated oversize boulders and logs into the building construction to match elements of the surrounding landscape. Longmire's Administration Building retains considerably more architectural integrity in its approach vista than Yosemite's. The Mount Rainier building was carefully sited at the end of an approach vista in an open area against a background of tall firs, cedars, and spruces. Barely perceptible is the subtle asymmetry of the main elevation to accommodate the off-center location of the one-story shed-roof entrance porch.

The building's exterior shows a highly refined composition of rustic elements executed with superb field skills and craftsmanship. The foundation, first-story, and second-story walls up to sill heights are composed of rounded glacial boulders. The battered glacial boulders flow upward from the ground

2b Longmire Community Building

2b Longmire Administration Building

in a careful plan of graduated sizes, achieving visual stability and emphasizing tapered lower wall windows with deep recesses. The upper story was veneered with horizontal logs, and the gable ends have contrasting vertical logs. Corners, visually strengthened by three massive vertical logs, draw the masonry of the lower story together with projecting rafters, eaves, and brackets of twelve-inch logs with whittled ends. The corner logs continue the visual pattern established in the entrance porch. The rhythm of casement windows grouped in threes capped with log lintels is identical on both floors. Thick cedar shakes extend this theme of solid construction, as does the log

2b Longmire Administration Building

ridgepole capping the roof. A boulder masonry chimney and a porch framed with logs complete the structure's exterior.

The approximately thirty-seven-by-sixty-eight-foot two-story plan contained all of the park's administrative staff in 1928. Although the room configuration has undergone a few slight changes, interior walls and finishes remain basically intact. A large glacial boulder fireplace is in the first-floor lobby; walls are of log-slab siding; windows and doors are framed out of massive logs with original hardware intact; wrought-iron chandeliers embellish the room and add to its rustic character.

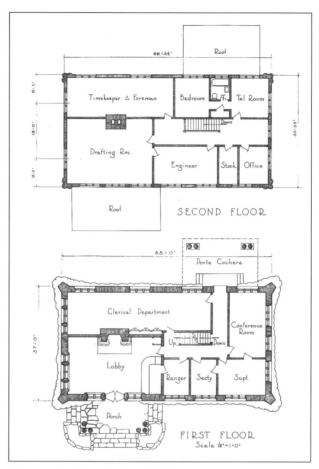

2b Longmire Administration Building

The Longmire Administration Building illustrates the maturing National Park Service philosophy of nonintrusive architecture in a glacial forest setting. Lower walls veneered with native stone, rise irregularly out of the earth. The massive logs used in the porch, upper story, and visible roof structure is proportional to the surrounding conifer forest. Plantings along the foundation walls establish yet another connection between the building and the forest. The Administration Building continued to function as the park headquarters until 1968, when the Mission 66 facility constructed outside the park at Tahoma Woods was completed. Today the building serves as a ranger station and center for maintenance operations in the park.

LONGMIRE SERVICE STATION

The third building of importance in this area is the Longmire Service Station, completed in 1929. Sited next to the National Park Inn on the approach road to the administration building, the service station is so well designed and nestled back into the trees that it is barely noticeable. Even its function does not seem incongruous within the forest setting. The National Park Service design staff managed to introduce local materials and ordinary features into the design for a building type that was simple but difficult to execute. Whole-log columns mounted on an island of glacial boulders and beams frame the overhanging porch and shelter the gas pumps while providing a one-lane drive-through. Walls of glacial boulders run up to windowsills sheathed with log half-rounds. Log corner posts match the overhang support columns. Windows on the first floor are multipane casement, and a single, square casement is placed in the gable end of the front elevation. The steeply pitched roof is covered with thick cedar-shake shingles.

2b Longmire Service Station

2c Paradise

When James Longmire's daughter-in-law first saw this subalpine meadow, she exclaimed, "This must be what Paradise is like." The road to Paradise climbs twenty-six hundred feet in thirteen miles of gentle grades and switchbacks from Longmire to Paradise Valley. Along the route, the road crosses Christine Falls Bridge. The fifty-six-foot span is one of the finest examples of a necessarily functional design that blends with the natural setting. Another example along the route is the Narada Falls Bridge, now used only for access to the Narada utility area.

As the traveler approaches Paradise, the cloud-wreathed snow-capped peak of Mount Rainier is an ever-expanding presence as the forest thins and alpine meadows with wildflowers come into view. The Cascade Range is arrayed to the south; snowcapped Mount Adams and Mount Hood and the truncated cone of Mount Saint Helens are visible on the horizon. The visitor center, a strikingly modern shallow-domed structure, hovers over the snowfields. A remnant of the Mission 66 architectural misadventures, it is a sharp contrast to the shake-covered walls and steeply pitched roofs of the Paradise Inn complex and National Park Service buildings.

The area known as Paradise resulted from a forest fire in 1885 that burned a thickly vegetated area on the western slope of Mount Rainier and left a stand of dead Alaskan cedars. Eventually, the dead limbs broke off and the charred bark wore away. Years of exposure weathered the cedars to a shimmering silver color, and the stand became known as the silver forest. It remained untouched for thirty-one years until National Park Service director Stephen Mather encouraged a group of Seattle and Tacoma businessmen to form a concession company for Mount Rainier and build a hotel in the silver forest area. He firmly believed in the dual mandate of the fledgling Park Service—preservation and use—and he felt that regulated concession companies in national parks would provide better control over the fragile natural resources. Paradise had been a popular Mount Rainier camping area for climbers and hikers since the nineteenth century, but the landscape was littered with a haphazard collection of tents and cottages. A better solution had to be found.

2c Paradise Inn, 1920s

PARADISE INN

Alert to the threat of outside developers, the local businessmen formed the Rainier National Park Company (RNPC) and financed construction of Paradise Inn in 1916. A site was selected—apparently an informal affair when the company's founders met at the end of the Paradise automobile road one spring day and hiked up to Paradise Valley, where they could see the summit of Mount Rainier, the Tatoosh Range, and the rest of the valley. They decided then and there that the location was perfect for their new hotel and winter sports resort.

The RNPC selected the Tacoma architectural firm of Heath, Gove, and Bell to design the hotel as the development's central feature. They also planned a large group of "bungalow" tents, a ski lift, and a guide house for the company's mountaineering service. Construction began during the summer of 1916, and the inn opened on July 1, 1917.

2c Paradise Inn, 1990s

Following the pattern established by concessioners in other "crown jewel" national parks, the RNPC set out to create a unique image for itself through its architecture. The company turned to the silver forest and harvested the well-seasoned timbers. The aged wood, with its silver patina, had obvious potential for unusual architectural effects. Reminiscent of Old Faithful Inn, the two-and-a-half-story inn has three steeply pitched roofs to shed the severe Cascade winter snows that average more than seven hundred inches annually. The huge gable roofs over the main lobby section and the dining room wing are more than two-thirds the height of the structure. This dominating architectural form makes the inn—in its isolated setting— seem particularly protective and sheltering. Dormers pierce the main roofs of the lobby and dining room sections, allowing light to penetrate into the deep interiors.

The lobby (approximately fifty by one-hundred-twelve feet) is the largest public space at Paradise Inn and a masterpiece of rustic framing and spatial architecture. The lobby is a delightful place for skiers, hikers, climbers,

2c Paradise Inn Lobby

2c Paradise Inn Dining Room

and other visitors. Fireplaces with huge stone chimneys, fifty and sixty feet high, warm each end of the lobby. Designers solved the problem of supporting the steeply pitched roof with a fine display of log-working skills used to assemble a pleasing rhythm of posts, beams, and trusses. The multilevel space is furnished with stout furniture and decorated with lanterns and Native American rugs. A second-story mezzanine (added in 1925) was wrapped around the lobby's upper portion—a place where visitors could sit at small writing tables to send letters or postcards home or just relax while people-watching and looking down on the scene below.

The fourteen lobby bays each had French doors facing north-northwest. The doors could be opened on warm days to let in the brisk alpine air and were easily boarded up for winter. Japanese lanterns, common in resort hotels like Glacier Park and El Tovar, originally lit the lobby; they were replaced with parchment-colored shades painted with pictures of local fauna.

An important decorative element in the lobby is the handcrafted Alaskan cedar furniture. During the winter of 1916–17, Hans Fraehnke,

2c Paradise Inn Annex

a creative German woodcrafter, lived at Paradise Inn. To help pass the time during the long winter, he crafted a piano, a grandfather clock, and probably the woodwork around the registration desk. The carefully carved quoins, spiky corner posts, and capping of broken pediment give the clock a sense of alpine grandeur. The piano, played by President Harry S. Truman during a visit, has heavy corner posts of peeled logs with pointed, whittled ends.

Four years after its construction, the RNPC decided to expand the inn. The magical warmth of the inn drew many visitors, but the bungalow tents proved to be less popular. In response to visitor demand, and with the approval of the National Park Service, the company constructed the Annex in 1920. The inn itself was generally T-shaped, and the Annex ran parallel to the larger wing of the main building, with a multistory enclosed bridge connecting the Annex to the inn. Subsequent changes included the addition of a mezzanine level in the lobby; construction of a new, larger kitchen wing; conversion of an enclosed porch off the rear of the lobby into a gift shop; and a porch added onto the south end of the building.

A Mission 66 prospectus evaluated Paradise Inn and, seeing the need for extensive maintenance work, recommended replacing it with a visitor center. Paradise Lodge, built in 1931, was purposely burned in 1965. However, many Washingtonians considered the inn such an important landmark that they refused to see it torn down. The inn was spared and the concessioner

2c Paradise Inn Lobby

began major renovations in 1980 to improve fire safety and structural stability. Work has included replacing the whole-log exterior buttresses with half logs that encase structural-steel members.

Paradise Inn still retains its original alpine character. Through the doors of the hostelry have passed movie stars, political dignitaries, and athletes participating in the 1936 Winter Olympic trials. Tyrone Power, Cecil B. DeMille, Sonja Henie, Harry S. Truman, the Crown Prince of Norway, and Shirley Temple warmed themselves by the hearth or sat quietly on the mezzanine level enjoying the space and observing the activity below. Today this architectural gem of the Pacific Northwest attracts thousands of people every year, who come to relax after a rigorous day's hiking or mountaineering or more gentle-paced enjoyment of the spectacular scenery.

GUIDE HOUSE

The RNPC constructed a guide-service building around 1920. Clever handling of the architectural form and materials was necessary to maintain compatibility with the nearby inn. Small in plan (thirty-two by seventy-four feet), it has a gambrel roof with dormers and exterior surfaces of Alaskan cedar shakes that effectively lower the scale of the tall narrow building. White pine log trim around the windows suggests a log frame, although the structure is timber-framed. Rainier Mountaineering, which leads climbs and provides training for rescue work, occupies the ground floor.

2c Paradise Guide House

NATIONAL PARK SERVICE BUILDINGS AT PARADISE

The National Park Service contributions to the Paradise Valley area include the Ranger Station, the ski-tow building, and the Comfort Station. Stephen Mather personally approved the plans for the ranger station, which

2c Paradise Ranger Station

was completed in 1922. Even though the use of stone was rejected by the concessioners as too labor-intensive, the National Park Service saw it as appropriate to Mount Rainier. Design experimentation is evident in the use of half logs at entrance doors and window surrounds and exposed first-floor log ceiling joists compared to milled lumber joists at the eaves. In later buildings, the National Park Service introduced log-roof framing to express a combination of structural and decorative elements.

The ski tow is a reminder of when Paradise Valley was one of the most popular ski areas in the Pacific Northwest, beginning in 1912. One of the early visitors, Miss Olive Rand, traveled on two long slabs of wood turned up at the ends and fastened to her feet with hoops, and explained that they were "skis." The National Park Service prohibited ski-tow facilities, but a portable lift was installed by the Civilian Conservation Corps in 1937. Although the inn was open only in summer months, skiers could use the shoulder seasons and hike in during winter months. The timber-framed, steeply pitched roof on the twelve-by-fourteen-foot lift structure was designed to blend with the ranger station and guide house.

The modest-sized Comfort Station, built in 1928, has an interesting design background. Rather than emphasize the facility and follow the pattern of steeply pitched roofs to shed the snow, the National Park Service chose a shallow-sloped roof on rubble-masonry walls to carry the heavy snow loads. The six-inch-thick reinforced-concrete slab was to be slate-covered, but substituting a tar-and-gravel roof reduced building costs.

2d Sunrise

Planning for the third and last major development of government and concession facilities in the park began in the late 1920s, when state highway construction authorities promised to open an approach from eastern Washington. The National Park Service was determined to avoid haphazard development that would endanger the fragile subalpine environment. Plans for Sunrise Village, to be built at Yakima Park, were prepared by the National Park Service Branch of Plans and Design in San Francisco under the supervision of Ernest A. Davidson. The National Park Service started work on an administrative/residential complex in 1930, while the RNPC began construction of a large hotel.

SUNRISE LODGE

The peculiar form and incomplete appearance of Sunrise Lodge is due to the concessioner's financial difficulties during the Great Depression. The fifty-seven-by-thirty-seven-foot barnlike structure is part of an original U-shaped plan. The RNPC's ambitious plans for Sunrise Lodge proceeded with construction of the first wing of the hotel in the spring of 1931, following a design modified by National Park Service architects to make it more compatible with the then-named Yakima Park (later renamed Sunrise) overall concept. Containing a dining room, kitchen, and employee facilities, Sunrise Lodge opened in mid-July 1931, with foundations in place for the second wing. Before beginning to build the lodging portion of the hotel, the concessioner laid out a tightly packed grid of 215 small guest cabins. As a result of financial difficulties in the early 1930s, the company never started the lodging portion and they sold off the cabins to farmers in eastern Washington for migrant-worker housing. The RNPC sold its holdings to the National Park Service in 1952.

The basement area in Sunrise Lodge now serves as a ranger station, the first floor functions as a cafeteria, as it did when it originally opened, and the upper floors are an employee dormitory. In contrast to the lodge, the small

2d Sunrise Lodge

2d Sunrise Lodge, detail

log-and-stone concessioner-built service station is an excellent example of rustic architecture. The low-silhouette battered-stone walls, log framing and trim, and gabled shake roof harmonize well with the subalpine setting.

YAKIMA PARK STOCKADE GROUP

In 1929, when the master plan for Yakima Park was prepared under Davidson's direction, the National Park Service was reaching the peak of its rustic-design strengths. The challenge here was to design buildings for administrative offices and visitor services in a completely undeveloped subalpine area at an elevation of 6,400 feet. The fragile ecosystem had to be taken into account, in addition to developing a design theme that would celebrate the magnificent views of Mount Rainier. A compact plan evolved that minimized both the impact of construction on the site and future unrestricted use of the site by visitors. Reviewing the project, Davidson showed great concern for the environmental impact, saying, "It is true that, purely from a landscape viewpoint, the whole development might be classified as a failure since the area is far less attractive than it was before the development took place. On the other hand, the project may be considered one of the great successes, since the general result obtained is far superior to those other developments with which comparison may be made, and which 'just grew,' like Topsy."

In sorting out design concepts for the project, Davidson turned to local sources of historical interest. A frontier blockhouse-and-stockade theme was developed from resource material at the Historical Museum of Tacoma. Architect A. Paul Brown completed the building designs in February 1930.

The master plan provided for a complete development at Yakima Park, including administrative offices, living quarters, campgrounds, trails, utility systems, and parking areas. In the headquarters area, plans called for a large Community Building, or Visitor Center, flanked by two square blockhouses. The National Park Service designers promoted a distinct style here, calling for carefully studied details in corner notching, overhung second floor, extended roof purlins, and chamfered log ends at the window jambs. A vertical stockade fence would enclose a utility yard behind the community building.

Plans were drawn so that construction could take place in three phases, but funding problems extended the project so that it was not completed until 1952. Initially, funds allowed for construction of only the South Blockhouse. In 1939 Public Works Administration funding was allocated for the construction of the North Blockhouse and Visitor Center. Again, capital

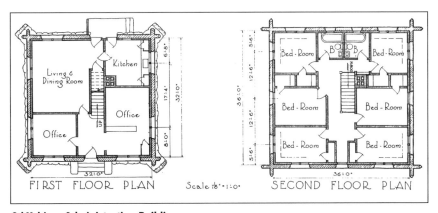

2d Yakima Administration Building

was exhausted, and these two structures were not completed until 1943. The visitor center acquired its stone-and-timber fireplace in 1952. The north blockhouse is similar to the south blockhouse, except for its more regular battered stonework.

The centerpiece of the complex is the Visitor Center; originally known as the "campers' shelter," it later became a museum/exhibit building. Seen from a distance, the three buildings blend together into the protective image of a frontier stockade. The three unattached blockhouses enclose a courtyard defined by the forms, textures, and tones of the surrounding walls. There is uniformity between rich textures and the reddish weathering of the building, which contrasts with the random whittled log-end projections. The buildings are visually unified by their stone foundations built to windowsill height, the carefully composed placement and proportions of window openings, and the consistent roof height.

The South Blockhouse, completed in 1931, recalls pioneer buildings built for protection. The two-story building is a cedar-log-framed structure

2d Yakima Park South Blockhouse, 1936

with saddle-notched corners and whittled log ends, and a hip roof of cedar shakes. Foundation stones are battered to the first floor windowsills "to reduce the squareness of the plan." The blockhouse character is enhanced by the second floor (thirty-eight feet on a side) overhanging the ground floor (thirty-two feet on a side) and the whole-log rafters projecting from the second floor.

The Visitor Center is a masterpiece of log construction designed to provide a large open interior (forty-two by eighty-eight feet). Lodgepole-pine log walls are drift-pin connected and saddle-notched to the roof plates at the corners. The interior open space required a long span of logs capable of supporting heavy snow loads. The ingenious solution rests log Pratt trusses across the room's width on log columns freestanding from the log walls. A pair of interior ridge beams carries log purlins and an exposed wooden-roof deck. Log knee braces provide additional support, and tie rods reinforce the trusswork. Carefully notched and coped, the supporting roof structure placed inside the log walls creates a dramatically rugged interior.

A subtle change is detected in the exterior log-wall construction of the Visitor Center, which has horizontal logs terminating at the second-floor overhang of the blockhouses. The entrance is defined by a pair of oversized log columns on either side of the door. Projecting square-cut rafter ends mark the simulated second floor, and a change of rhythm occurs with vertical log sheathing placed between the clerestory windows. Log walls are saddle-notched at the corners, and whittled rafter log ends project under the eaves in harmony with the blockhouses. The gable roof is covered with cedar shakes, and a ridge log overhangs both gable ends.

Clerestory windows bring in light through the east and west walls; a large picture window on the south wall looks out on Mount Rainier. On sunny days, crowds cluster at the window to watch climbers on the mountain's northeast slope. A coursed, oversized stone fireplace at the north end of the room is framed with log columns and beams.

The usually understated *Park and Recreation Structures* deemed the stockade group a design success: "Even without the magnificent backdrop of Mount Rainier this log building [the south blockhouse] would be an outstanding contribution to park architecture. Obviously, but not too self-consciously, inspired by the early blockhouse, here is a building representative of a logical and legitimate adaptation of a traditional form. The log work is neither too precise nor too laboriously rustic."

The success of Sunrise is due to its setting; for the simple forms, resting on a grassy slope surrounded by subalpine vegetation with the imposing presence of snow-covered Mount Rainier in the background give the complex a wild, frontier appearance.

2d Yakima Park Stockade, with detail

2e Bridges

Road building to connect entrances and main park features produced National Park Service designs of outstanding rustic-style bridges that gracefully merged with the landscape. Locations are dramatic, spanning deep gorges with waterfalls and rushing streams. Faced with massive native-stone voussoirs and broken-range masonry, a reinforced-concrete single arch and three centered arches are of various structural configurations: barrel arches covered with earth fill; arched concrete girders; and arched concrete T-beams. Bridges were sited at carefully selected crossing points where construction could harmonize with adjacent natural granite outcroppings.

The often-photographed Narada Falls and Christine Falls Bridges on the road from Longmire to Paradise, both built in 1927–28, nimbly span picturesque gorges and waterfalls on roughly cut, stone-faced concrete arches. The twenty-foot-wide, two-lane Narada Falls Bridge is a flat arched bridge of five reinforced concrete girders, cross-beams, and deck with a clear span of thirty-six feet. Christine Falls Bridge is a three-centered, earth-filled, reinforced-concrete barrel arch. The fifty-six-foot clear span has a thirty-foot-wide roadway. A facing of stone voussoirs and arch-and-spandrel wall masonry merge with the gorge's side walls. The bridge is on a gentle curve and an adjacent parking area leads down a trail to a falls overlook.

Other examples of finely designed rustic-style bridges are the South Puyallup River and St. Andrews Creek Bridges on the Westside Road, the White River Bridge on the White River–Yakima Park Road, and the Muddy Creek Bridge at Box Canyon on the Stevens Canyon Road.

Olympic National Park

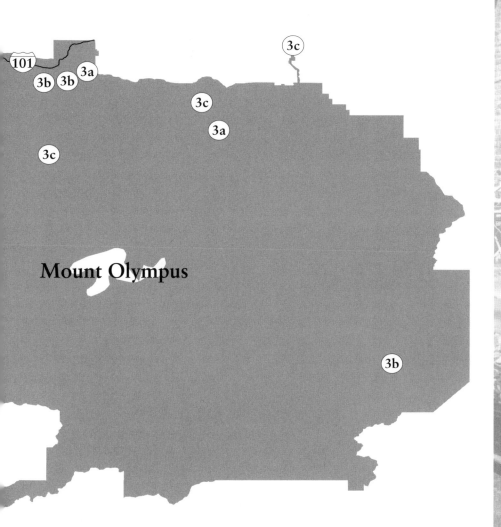

101

3b 3b 3a

3c

3c

3a

3c

Mount Olympus

3b

3b Lake Crescent Lodge Lobby

3 Olympic National Park
Clallam, Jefferson, and Mason Counties, Washington
www.nps.gov/olym

Driving from the Seattle/Tacoma via ferries and the Hood Canal Bridge, it takes two-and-a-half to three hours to reach Port Angeles, location of the main visitor center and park headquarters. U.S. Highway 101 provides the main access to the park from the Seattle-Tacoma area, with numerous spur roads leading inland following drainages to trailheads that access six hundred miles of hiking trails. No roads cross through the interior of the park. The coast area can be reached directly from U.S. 101 at Kalaloch and from spur roads to the mouth of the Hoh, to La Push, and to Rialto Beach.

■ "Of all the national parks, the most diversified in character and climate is Olympic. Here you will find seacoast and mountain peak, rain forest and glacier, and an unbelievable abrupt change of weather pattern."
Dorothy N. Krell (editor), *National Parks of the West*

Olympic National Park, in the center of the northwestern corner of Washington State's Olympic Peninsula, contains three distinctly different ecosystems—seashore, rugged glacier-capped mountains, and magnificent stands of old-growth and temperate rain forests. The land rises gently from the waters of the Pacific, the Strait of Juan de Fuca, and Puget Sound, then steepens abruptly into a tight circular cluster of peaks. The summit of Mount Olympus rises to almost eight thousand feet. Below the jagged peaks and timberline, a network of thirteen rivers threads its way down to sea level. Rain forests, thick stands of conifers, deep-cut rivers, mountain streams pouring through alpine meadows, and lakes and shorelines provide an ecological haven worthy of its recent designation as a World Biosphere Park.

The 922,000-acre park (with almost 877,000 acres in wilderness area) is divided into two parts: a sixty-three-mile strip of coast, and the inland block of forest, valley, meadow, and mountain. The wet western area contains up-and-down country full of peaks and ridges, where moisture-laden air from the Pacific Ocean becomes trapped; the dry eastern side is marked by a series of peaks separated by short, steep river canyons. The western side of the park has the wettest climate in the lower forty-eight states, with nearly twelve feet of precipitation annually. The northern side is the driest part of the Pacific Coast outside of Southern California. Almost 95 percent of the park is designated wilderness.

Discovery and Settlement

The Olympic Peninsula, and especially its mountain core, has always been a remote isolated place. Although less than one hundred miles from Seattle, this wilderness for many years hindered settlement. Native American tribes originally populated the coast and interior river areas, and continue to do so.

Early reports of this region date back to late-sixteenth-century explorers. Spanish and English mariners, including Captain James Cook, sailed these waters seeking a Northwest Passage to connect the Atlantic and Pacific Oceans. Russian expeditions joined the British at the end of the eighteenth century in the pursuit of fur. At the same time, American expeditions were organized to explore the coast. The mysterious mountainous interior of the peninsula lured trappers and traders during the first half of the 1800s. After hearing reports from the Lewis and Clark expedition, the Hudson's Bay Company and U.S. ventures became interested in the area.

The first organized and publicized accounts of general public travel in the Olympic Range occurred in the late 1800s. Several parties crossed the peninsula, and their exploits were widely circulated in the regional and national press. A resolve quickly emerged that the unspoiled mountains and wilderness should be preserved as a national park, a distinction shared by only a few of the original national parks.

Federal management of the region began in 1897, when President McKinley established the Olympic Forest Reserve covering two-thirds of the Olympic Peninsula. However, mining interests prevailed and the Reserve was restored to public domain in 1900 and enlarged in 1907. In 1909 President Theodore Roosevelt declared Mount Olympus National Monument of 615,000 acres to protect Olympic elk, or "Roosevelt" elk, and some of the splendid forests. After almost forty argumentative years during which the region passed through various identities, it became established as Olympic National Park in 1938. Administration shifted between the Department of Agriculture and the Department of the Interior. The park has fluctuated from the Forest Service's initial 615,000 acres down to a low of 300,000 acres in 1915, and up to its present 922,650 acres. Its boundaries have been adjusted a half-dozen times, with the coastal strip added in 1953.

Struggles with lumbering interests account for most of the park's difficulties. Proponents for preserving the wilderness prevailed, arguing that creating a national park would yield long-term benefits to the entire country and outweigh the short-term benefits to the local economy. But the fight to save the forests became a protracted battle, moving in and out of congressional committees, engaging the president's cabinet, and even drawing President Franklin D. Roosevelt to Port Angeles, Washington, in 1937 in an attempt to settle the disputed issues. The park was legislated into existence in 1938, and attempts to alter its federal protection status were rejected during the war years and again in later years when local congressional representatives renewed the issue.

3a Historic Structures

Discovering the historic structures in Olympic National Park may involve an automobile trip to a specific resort, a long drive to a remote trailhead, or the serendipitous discovery of a shelter, cabin, or chalet along a hiking trail. Because of natural deterioration and park administration decisions to remove specific structures, all the nineteenth-century structures in the park have vanished. The twentieth-century buildings, retaining their integrity in stunning settings, are precious cultural resources.

There are more than 110 structures contained in the National Park Service List of Classified Structures that serve as an interpretive resource for the history of Olympic National Park. Insights into the park's identity are found at the Humes Cabin (1900), the Storm King Ranger Station (1905), the Park Headquarters (1940), and the buildings that were put up either by early settlers, through recreation development, or by Great Depression–era relief programs. Backcountry trails and shelters, private chalets, lakeside and hot springs resorts, housekeeping cabins, and auto campgrounds on lakes and streams—all had their day and left their mark. They provided a certain level of safety and comfort for people who wanted to venture cautiously into the wilderness.

When the Forest Service developed trails, shelters, and chalets on the peninsula, it promoted the public's early interest and participation in the backcountry, which inspired the popular support essential to the creation of Olympic National Park. The frontcountry lakeshore, coastal beach, hot springs resort, and campgrounds also attracted large numbers of visitors, who were exposed to a very different version of the wilderness experience. Under Forest Service and National Park Service supervision, work-relief programs such as the Civilian Conservation Corps, dedicated to expanding and improving park facilities, strengthened the appeal of both the frontcountry and backcountry. The National Park Service summarized the dualism of the popular, more accessible portions of the park with the remote interior when it stated, "This increasingly popular sense of the need for wild and quiet places both supported and threatened the Olympic National Park resources it most highly respected."

Olympic National Park historic structures show a remarkable consistency in materials and design. Whether this was conscious or accidental, private as well as public buildings were built on a scale and with materials appropriate for their surroundings. Dictated by the availability of local materials and labor, log or drop-channel siding, shingle or shake roofs, and small-pane wood-framed windows prevail. Locations respect rather than dominate sites. Widely differing objectives follow these themes, from cabin to Forest Service shelter to private resort or chalet.

Construction from 1925 to 1929 of trail systems, ranger stations, fire caches, and shelters were based on Forest Service plans. Although the

National Park Service did not begin managing the region until Olympic National Park was created in 1938, after that time it closely followed the widely disseminated National Park Service design guidelines laid out in *Park Structures and Facilities.* When the Civilian Conservation Corps (CCC), Public Works Administration (PWA), or Work Projects Administration (WPA) relief programs built new structures in the park, they followed earlier Forest Service designs and National Park Service rustic-design principles both to minimize intrusions and "design them [so] that, besides being attractive to look upon, they appear to belong to and be a part of their settings."

Humes Ranch Cabin

Set at the edge of a meadow against a tree line, Humes Ranch Cabin is one of the few remaining homestead structures intact on the Olympic

3a Humes Ranch Cabin

3a Humes Ranch Cabin, details

Peninsula. The oldest cabin in Olympic National Park, it is a solitary structure of log construction with a cedar-shake roof. Originally built in 1900 and restored in 1980, the cabin displays precisely cut dovetail corner joints and hemp chinking.

Will Humes, along with a brother and a cousin, went from New York to Washington State seeking gold. Disappointed by their mining attempts, the Humes family nonetheless found the plentiful fish and game and good pastureland appealing. In 1900 Will and a third brother, Grant, built their log cabin two-and-a-half miles south of the Whiskey Bend trailhead. Will returned East in 1916, but Grant stayed on at the cabin until his death in 1934. Commenting on his reasons for remaining in that solitary wet place, Grant wrote Will his observations from a 1928 visit to Seattle: "The life they lead has no attraction for me and I am glad to get back to the cool, green wood and the peace and quiet and beauty to be enjoyed there."

Grant's subsistence-farming life was supplemented by guiding packing parties, including the first group ascent of Mount Olympus. The resourceful Humes men developed a homestead that expanded into a complex of barns and sheds to lodge summer and fall packing parties. Gable-roofed and rectangular in shape, the Humes cabin is typical of early homestead residences.

The builders turned to the streambeds and forests for their major building materials: stone for foundations, logs for the walls, and cedar shakes for the roofs. Window sash and dimensioned lumber might have come from the nearest lumber mill. Porches often were built across the cabin front to extend interior living space and provide shelter from the peninsula weather. Windows were used sparingly. Fireplaces were rare, and heat generally was provided by woodstoves with flue pipes extending through the roof. The gable roof has a welcoming hip-roofed porch supported by peeled poles. One can easily picture Grant Humes standing on the porch, a dog at his side, looking over a tarpaulin-covered collection of pack luggage as he prepared his guests for an adventurous trip along the mountain trails of the Elwha River.

STORM KING INFORMATION STATION

The Storm King Information Station at Barnes Point on Lake Crescent is one of the few buildings remaining in the park that date from the early days of federal administration. In the early 1890s, when Chris Morgenroth settled near the Bogachiel River close to the park's current western boundary,

3a Storm King Information Station, 1935; detail (p. 233)

239

he was in the company of a dozen other homesteaders. When the Olympic Forest Reserve was created in 1897, the settlers' freedom to cut timber was restricted, and the lack of access roads ended many of their dreams. In 1905 Morgenroth joined the Forest Service, moved to the Barnes Point site, and built a cabin that originally served as the first Forest Service ranger station on the Peninsula. After 1938 the National Park Service used the cabin as a ranger station, patrol cabin, employee residence, and today as the Storm King Information Station.

The two-story cabin, approximately twenty-five by thirty feet in plan, was constructed of horizontal log walls with cross-notched corners on a post-and-pier foundation. A slate stone fireplace, interior walls of knotty cedar, and tongue-and-groove flooring augmented the owner's comfortable lifestyle. The steeply pitched cedar-shake-shingle gable roof with two dormers, the porch on peeled-pole logs across the front of the cabin, the generous window openings, and the well-crafted construction suggest a greater sense of permanency than many other structures in the park. This was a residence for a family independent of the land.

3b Resorts and Lodges

Beginning in the 1890s vacationers spread across the peninsula and created a market for resort lodgings. The coastline, lake shorelines, hot springs, and remote valleys hosted the growing urban middle class seeking a wilderness experience. When the loop highway was completed in 1931, older resorts expanded to accommodate the growing numbers of automobiles. Many of the first resorts were lost to fire, one to an avalanche, and at least two to levels of success that dictated near-total replacement.

Although most of the early resort hotels bordering the shores of Lake Crescent are gone, two resort complexes dating from the lake's heyday during the Forest Reserve's first twenty years are still standing. Located at Barnes Point, Singer's Tavern (now the Lake Crescent Lodge) and Rosemary Inn both opened in 1915. Separated by only a few hundred yards of thick forest, the two resorts evoke the scale, setting, and landscaping of an earlier era.

Outside the park boundaries, on the south shore of Lake Quinault, the Quinault Lodge suggests the more elegant style of accommodations that were once available in the park. Located in the park's interior, Sol Duc Hot

3b Barnes Point at Lake Crescent

Springs was a large resort for people drawn to the therapeutic waters. The original buildings were destroyed by fire four years after opening, and the modern replacement is of ordinary functional design. Only one resort remains in existence in the backcountry. A successful preservation story surrounds the Enchanted Valley Chalet, opened in 1931 and recently rebuilt by volunteers.

Lake Crescent Lodge

Twelve-mile-long Lake Crescent was one of the first sites in Olympic National Park to be developed as a resort area. About twenty miles west of Port Angeles, rough trails opened-up the lake in the early 1890s to travelers attracted by the scenery of the surrounding three-thousand-to-four-thousand-foot ridges and peaks. Plentiful lake trout, an impressive setting, and a chance to explore an edge of the rugged peninsula created a demand for tourist accommodations.

A rough log-cabin hotel opened in 1891 and a steam launch, *The Lady of the Lake,* provided tours around the lake. A burgeoning resort area soon developed, with several hotels offering attractive lodgings, spacious and well-furnished public rooms, gardens, and recreation areas. Resorts like the Log

241

3b Lake Crescent Lodge

Cabin Hotel, the Fairholme, the Marymere, the Qui Si Sana, and the Lake Crescent Hotel were all built before World War II. All have since vanished, destroyed by fire or removed by the National Park Service.

Lake Crescent Lodge opened at Barnes Point as Singer's Tavern in 1915. The most distinctive feature of the two-story-frame main lodge is the glass-enclosed front porch facing the lake. Al Singer's lodge kept growing until thirty cottages complemented the main lodge. Modern motel accommodations were added in the 1950s. Guests arrived by ferry until 1922, when the first road around the lake's southern shore was completed. The Singers and later owners made improvements to the original buildings, eventually adding electricity and running water to the cabins.

The two-story shingled, wood-frame main lodge's character remains essentially unchanged, although substantially rehabilitated in the 1980s. A wide verandah provides shelter for the entrance. The lobby and main public room's comfortable Arts & Crafts furniture, board-and-batten walls, bric-a-brac, and memorabilia on tables and walls provide a cozy greeting for travelers. A rubble-stone fireplace with a mounted Roosevelt elk head above warms the lodge on chilly days. Only five of the ten second-floor rooms sharing a common bath are open to the public, but they provide superb views of the lake, forests, and ridges.

PRESIDENTIAL VISIT

Few lodges in the national park system have enjoyed the distinction of a president's visit. A party led by President Franklin D. Roosevelt, with cabinet officers, congressmen, Park Service officials, Washington State political leaders, and prominent journalists, gathered at Lake Crescent Lodge in 1937 to reconcile differing opinions about whether or not a national park ought to be established for the surrounding area. Roosevelt stayed in one of the "fireplace cabins," which are original lodge structures. The Roosevelt charm, aided by a White House conference and a special message to Congress the following April, laid the groundwork for successful passage of the bill creating Olympic National Park.

ROSEMARY INN

"Quaint" and "charming" describe the meadow setting of Rosemary Inn. The main lodge and cabin names—Cara Mia, Dreamerie, Summerie, Dixie, Alabam, Honeysuckle, Silver Moon, Rock-A-Bye, Dardanella, and Red Wing—reflect Rose Littleton's care and hospitality in creating this enclave, which she began in 1915. (By combining her first name with that

3b Rosemary Inn, Summerie Cabin

3b Rosemary Inn, Main Lodge, 1930s

3b Rosemary Inn, Main Lodge

of her lifelong partner, Mary Daum, the "Rose" and "Mary" became
"Rosemary.") The fascination of Rosemary Inn lies in the timelessness of the
sheltered setting and simple buildings, recalling the days of travel on unpaved
roads through the peninsular rain forests.

3b Rosemary Inn Entrance

Guests, arriving by ferry across Lake Crescent, were welcomed by a tall, rustic, peeled-pole gateway decorated with latticework and "Rosemary" in large peeled-stick letters. Rows of canvas tents were arranged on either side of the meadow as lodgings. Over a period of five to fifteen years, cabins were built to replace the tents. Mary Daum's brother, John Daum, was an excellent craftsman who designed and built all of the structures. Rose Littleton cultivated a large garden area along the meadow's edge, planting fruit trees, shrubs, and flower gardens. Trellises were built and fountains were added to enhance the landscape design. The one-and-one-half-story main lodge evolved with additions altering the rectangular floor plan, the dormers, and the porches.

The visitor finds no coherent organization to the randomly sited cabins. Much of the delight in Rosemary Inn comes from the almost whimsical mixture of building forms, materials, and the sequence of charmingly named cabins. Two of the original buildings were of log construction; the others were wood-framed. Remnants of the original groomed lawns and formal landscaping can be seen in the three stone-and-concrete fountains and an occasional exotic shrub.

The best way to view the cabins is by strolling through the meadow

3b Rosemary Inn, Red Wing Cabin

3b Rosemary Inn, Dreamerie Cabin

toward the shoreline. Mostly of wood-frame construction on post-and-pier foundations, this group of cabins contains no twins. Each is unique in design, no larger than fifteen by twenty feet in plan, L-shaped or rectangular, with extended porches and sheds. The eclectic whimsy of design continues with the sheathing materials, which include horizontal clapboards, vertical board and batten, wood shingles, cedar bark, and stucco. A bay window here, a diamond-shaped casement window there, porch-roof brackets of peeled logs, jerkinhead roofs—unexpected building elements are found at every turn. Each cabin is identified by a small signboard over the entrance. A three-sided shelter of peeled-log construction sits at the edge of the meadow by the shoreline.

Rosemary Inn was the setting for two historic moments in park history. During President Roosevelt's visit to nearby Lake Crescent Lodge in 1937, the presidential party breakfasted at Rosemary Inn. Nine years later, it was the setting for the Olympic National Park dedication ceremony, led by Secretary of the Interior Julius A. Krug. In 1943 the National Park Service acquired the property to operate as a concession. Rosemary Inn was placed on the National Register of Historic Places in 1979. The complex is now used for the Olympic Park Institute headquarters and its wide range of environmental programs. Modern bunkhouses are set in the woods.

ENCHANTED VALLEY CHALET

The Valley of a Thousand Waterfalls, the original name of Enchanted Valley, catches the rare quality of the hundred-acre meadow surrounded by mountains and a two thousand-foot wall of rock to the north. In wet seasons, waterfalls cascade over the rocky precipices. The five Olson brothers of Hoquiam, Washington, had formed a hiking and trail-guide service in the late 1920s and vied for the right to develop the North Fork of the Quinault River. They were turned down and searched elsewhere for a chalet site. The Forest Service invited a proposal from them in 1929 for the Enchanted Valley location, approximately seventeen miles from the trailhead at Dosewallips. The Olsons' application was approved, and construction of the Enchanted Valley Chalet began in 1931.

The log building measures twenty-eight by forty feet and follows the Forest Service guidelines for "architect's plans embodying a harmonious design either in rustic, Swiss chalet or other suitable style." The building was framed with locally cut, full-length, squared cedar logs, which end in diagonal-cut dovetail joints. Minor rustic touches were added with peeled-pole purlins and supporting braces for the overhanging roof at the gable ends. Two small shed roofs over the entrances are recent additions. Bricks and mortar for the chimney, disassembled window frames and sashes, and milled lumber for interiors were hauled to the site by packhorses. Interiors have tongue-and-groove flooring throughout, peeled-pole ceiling joists, and exposed pole rafters in the attic. There are three rooms on the first floor, including a kitchen, bedroom, and living room; six sleeping rooms on the second floor; and a large room in the attic. Walls are made of flattened log faces running vertically. After a water system was added in 1934, a bathtub was brought into the valley behind a packhorse and installed on the second floor.

The chalet was a favorite stopping place for hikers and horse caravans during the 1930s. On a thirteen-mile pack trip through the Olympics, the fifth day brought a party to Enchanted Valley. The prospect of a fireplace, cooks, good food, beds, and a bath were as welcome a sight as the spectacular setting. After incorporation into the park, the Olympic Recreation Company owners decided to sell their holdings to the National Park Service, who kept it in operation until 1943, when it was manned by the Aircraft Warning Service. By 1951 the National Park Service had finally consummated the purchase, and the chalet was put back in operation in 1953.

The final chapter in the history of Enchanted Valley Chalet is a happy one. A hiking club from Hoquiam (the Olympians) and the National Park Service worked to stabilize and restore it after several years of decay and vandalism. With volunteer labor and National Park Service guidance, the welcoming chalet is once again available for travelers into Enchanted Valley. The chalet serves as a reminder of private commercial efforts to develop recreational opportunities in Olympic's interior wilderness and plays an important role in the park's interpretive history.

3b Enchanted Valley Chalet

3c The Federal Influence: The Civilian Conservation Corps, Shelters, and Headquarters

Soon after the Forest Service took over management of Olympic Forest Reserve in 1905, plans were laid to open the interior wilderness for recreation. Administration by the National Park Service, which began in 1938, followed after forty years of Forest Service management of the Olympic National Forest. Overlapping the transition from one federal agency to another, there was a brief period of enormous activity (1933–42) when funds and labor were available through federal work-relief programs.

A variety of structures—ranger stations, trail shelters, and outbuildings—reflect the Forest Service's concern for preserving wilderness through multiple-resource management. The need to provide access to timber and a concern for forest-fire prevention and control led to the development of a comprehensive trail system. The original system of trails, houses, and shelters conceived for Forest Service use would also provide access to the interior of the Olympic Peninsula for a growing number of hiking, hunting, and fishing enthusiasts.

By the mid-1930s, six hundred miles of trails and more than one hundred shelters had been constructed on the peninsula. Built of readily available logs and split-cedar shakes, the simple structures were based on Adirondack shelter design: open on one side with a peeled-pole log frame, a roof with two unequal pitches lowers over the rear wall and sharply to the front, split-shake walls and roofs, and a dirt floor. The shelters were spaced along the trails at reasonable hiking distances and became part of the Forest Service promotion of recreational opportunities in the reserve.

Design and placement of the shelters adhered to Forest Service principles of preserving the primitive wilderness: "Building should be in the way of such Forest Service improvements as are absolutely necessary. . . . Other buildings beyond such rough shelters as may be considered necessary should be kept out." Of the fewer than thirty extant shelters, only a handful have not been altered by maintenance crews, who changed exteriors to board-and-batten siding and added raised wooden floors. The best examples are found along the Bogachiel River in the Hoh subdistrict. An inspired peeled-log structure in the rustic style of the National Park Service is the Soleduck Falls Shelter (1939). National Park Service rustic work is also illustrated by the

3c Elwha Shelter Kitchen

3c Elwha Ranger Station, detail

3c Elwha Ranger Station

Civilian Conservation Corps–built Elwha Shelter Kitchen and Altaire Shelter. Ranger stations at Elwha, Altaire, Elkhorn, North Fork, Quinault, and Staircase are simple designs in "Forest Service Rustic"—functional clapboard siding incorporating the pine-tree symbol of both the Forest Service and the Civilian Conservation Corps in the gable ends.

Elwha Ranger Station and Campgrounds

The Elwha Ranger Station and nearby Campgrounds contain groupings of structures that illustrate the transition from Forest Service to Civilian Conservation Corps building in the park. The Ranger Station is a complex of sixteen buildings from the early 1930s, although the wood-frame structures with clapboard, shake, or half-log siding exteriors and casement windows did follow the Forest Service's dictates for aesthetically pleasing as well as substantial buildings compatible with their surroundings.

These buildings might well be said to follow the bungalow style, a common residential design of the 1930s, but are slightly embellished with heavy, squared-timber porch supports and brackets. The Civilian Conservation Corps touch is evident in the decorative pine-tree design cut into shutters, porch railings, and gable-end boards. The Elwha Ranger Station complex serves as a reminder of the Forest Service's unobtrusive design style, and the buildings in this grouping are substantially the same as they were more than sixty years ago.

The Elwha and Altaire Campgrounds, the first a mile north of the ranger station and the second a mile south, contain the two examples of Civilian Conservation Corps community kitchens that survive in the park. The Elwha Kitchen is an octagonal, open-sided roofed pavilion with a central stone-masonry fireplace and chimney. It was built in 1935 with oversized peeled-log columns and an exposed purlin roof covered with shake shingles. Original railings have been removed, but the framing notches are still visible; the original shelter is otherwise intact.

SOLEDUCK FALLS SHELTER

Less than a mile from the Soleduck River trailhead, the Civilian Conservation Corps built one of three rustic log shelters in the park. This fine example of workmanship and design, and the only remaining Civilian Conservation Corps shelter, was completed in 1939. Workers from the Elwha

3c Soleduck Falls Shelter

Civilian Conservation Corps camp provided labor for the project, which was in a wooded setting on a high bank thirty feet from the Soleduck River.

Unlike the Forest Service's typical Adirondack lean-to design, the Soleduck Falls Shelter's more elaborate rustic form in logs shows the influence of the distinctive design, attention to detail, use of native building materials, quality of workmanship, and nonintrusive siting that are hallmarks of National Park Service rustic design. A heroically proportioned ten-by-ten-foot entrance portico is at the front of the eleven-by-twenty-one-foot main building. The portico's shake roof, supported on peeled-log columns with exposed-log lintels and purlins, joins the shelter's main-roof ridge to create a cross-gable roof. A small clerestory, supported on peeled log poles and covered by a shake roof, is perched at the midpoint of the portico's roof. A wide opening in the shelter's log wall provides access to the interior. Horizontal log walls with saddle-notched joints and projecting corners form the walls; vertical half-logs were used to close in the gable ends.

The sensitivity of the design and quality of the workmanship in this simple structure are highlighted by the subtlety of intersecting forms and the projecting log ends. The shelter's main log walls end in a horizontal wedge shape, roof purlins are pointed, and gable logs end in a lancet shape. The Soleduck Falls Shelter is an excellent example of the craftsmanship practiced by the Civilian Conservation Corps prior to, and during, the formative years of Olympic National Park.

PARK HEADQUARTERS

A high priority for the newly created Olympic National Park was the building of the Administrative Headquarters. A location was selected at Peabody Heights in Port Angeles, four miles from the park's main northern boundary, and with Work Projects Administration funds allocated to the National Park Service, the first five buildings of the sixteen-building complex were completed in 1941.

Construction at the site, supervised by both the Project Works Administration and Civilian Conservation Corps proceeded slowly at first. Continuous rainfall delayed excavation work, and then there were delays in obtaining materials. A lack of qualified stonemasons and the cost of skilled labor quickly put the project over budget. Additional funds were procured and the first two structures, the Administration Building and the Superintendent's Residence, were ready for occupancy by June 1940.

253

3d Park Headquarters Building

As is the case for several other Olympic National Park buildings, the Park Headquarters complex is of greater interest for its interpretive history than as an example of distinctive architecture. By 1940 the National Park Service rustic-design tradition was in eclipse. The "exaggerated rustic" look was disappearing in favor of more contemporary trends. It was replaced with only minor concessions to immediate settings and most typically with unexceptional wood-frame houses incorporating rustic siding and stone-veneer walls. The National Park Service's design philosophy retained its principle of nonintrusive architecture, but modern functionalism with simpler, more efficient design replaced the old order.

The Park Headquarters building illustrates a shift in National Park Service design taste from rustic to modernistic elements, a transitional building between rustic and Mission 66. The forty-six-by-eighty-seven-foot two-story wood-frame building has a ground floor of wood-framed stone veneer that provides a strong monolithic base for a lighter, wood-framed second floor sheathed with smaller-scaled shingles. Logs projecting over the stone base provided structural support for the upper floor to emphasize its lightness. Door and window openings are designed to maintain the integrity of horizontal layers contrasted with stone and shingle.

3 Michael's Cabin, with detail

The historic architecture in Olympic National Park is a modest collection, subordinate to the rich variety of place. Buildings alongside trails or lakeshores are selective remnants of the park's history and are reminders of the exploration, commercial development, recreation, federal management, and relief programs that have taken place in it. As one discovers a cabin or trailside shelter, a resort hotel or ranger station, the desire to classify a building by its role in interpretive history is lost in the simple act of discovery. After hours of hiking through the wilderness, the sighting of one of these structures is a poignant reminder that in this region weather dominates, and people and buildings are transient. John Muir may have had the Olympic Peninsula in mind when he wrote, "Come to the woods, for here is rest. . . . Of all the upness accessible to mortals, there is no upness compared to the mountains."

San Juan Island
National Historical Park

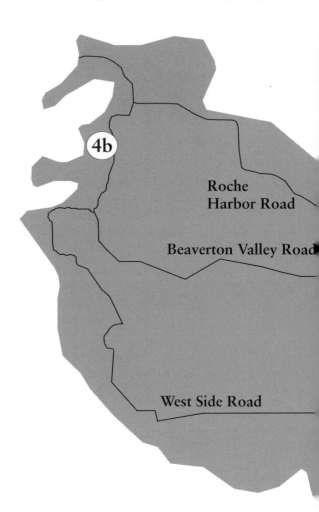

Roche
Harbor Road

Beaverton Valley Road

West Side Road

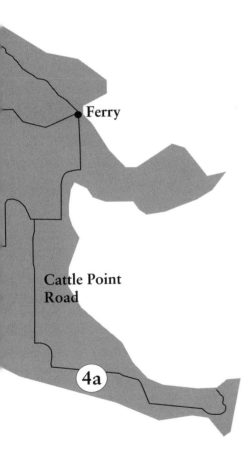

Ferry

Cattle Point
Road

4a

4b (above) English Camp from Young Hills above the cemetery, Cuss Island center left; (below) plot plan of the remains of Old English Camp; (facing) detail of barracks

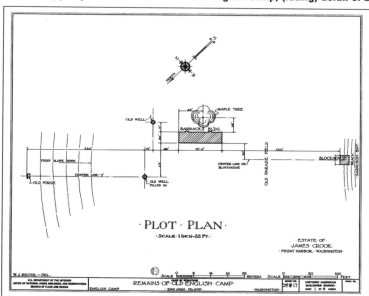

· PLOT · PLAN ·

· SCALE · 1 INCH=32 FT. ·

· ESTATE · OF ·
· JAMES · CROOK ·
· FRIDAY HARBOR · WASHINGTON ·

W.J MEYER ~ DEL.

U.S. DEPARTMENT OF THE INTERIOR
OFFICE OF NATIONAL PARKS, BUILDINGS, AND RESERVATIONS
BRANCH OF PLANS AND DESIGN

ENGLISH CAMP

REMAINS · OF · OLD · ENGLISH · CAMP ·
· SAN JUAN · ISLAND · · WASHINGTON ·

HISTORIC AMERICAN
BUILDINGS SURVEY
SHEET 1 OF 5 SHEETS

·NORTHEAST· ELEVATION·
· SCALE-¼INCH-1 FOOT·

4 San Juan Island National Historical Park
Whatcom County, Washington

www.nps.gov/sajh

The park is located on an island accessible by Washington State Ferry from Anacortes, Washington, eighty-three miles north of Seattle, or from Sydney, British Columbia, fifteen miles north of Victoria. Park visitor centers are located at American Camp, six miles southeast of Friday Harbor, and English Camp, about nine miles northeast of Friday Harbor.

■ "It would be a shocking event if . . . two nations should be precipitated into a war respecting the possession of a small island . . . over a squabble about a pig."

Admiral Robert L. Baynes, commander of British forces in the Pacific

In June 1859 the Americans and the British almost went to war over a boundary dispute on this island and a pig. The 1,751-acre San Juan Island National Historic Park, established on September 9, 1966, commemorates the events on the island from 1853 to 1871—the final settlement of the

Oregon Territory's boundary and the peaceful resolution of the killing of a British pig by an American settler. The incident came to be known as the "Pig War."

The park consists of two units protecting the remains of the British and American encampments. The English Camp at Garrison Bay at the northwest end of the island has restored barracks and blockhouse, commis-

4b English Camp, as seen today

sary, hospital, and formal garden. The American Camp on the island's southeastern tip has two original buildings, officers' quarters and a laundress quarters, and the remains of the redoubt, an earthen gun emplacement. Volunteers conduct historical reenactments in period clothes on Saturday afternoons during the summer months.

The dispute actually began when the Treaty of 1846 gave the United States undisputed possession of the Pacific Northwest south of the forty-ninth parallel, extending the boundary "to the middle of the channel which separates the continent from Vancouver Island; and thence southerly through the middle of said channel, and of Fuca's straits to the Pacific Ocean." But while the treaty settled the larger boundary question, it left unclear who owned San Juan Island. Both nations claimed this island and both encouraged settlement to support their respective claims.

By 1859 the Hudson's Bay Company had established a salmon-curing station and a sheep ranch there, and about twenty-five Americans settled on redemption claims. It was a volatile situation and reached a crisis when an American settler, Lyman Cutlar, shot and killed a Hudson's Bay Company pig because it was rooting in his garden. Hostilities quickly escalated. Fortunately, cooler heads prevailed. A standoff with joint occupancy of the island lasted twelve years until Kaiser Wilhelm I of Germany, acting as head of an international arbitration committee, ruled that the boundary lay west of the island. On October 21, 1872, the Pig War was settled, with the only casualty being the pig, and San Juan Island belonged to the United States. In November 1872 the Royal Marines withdrew from the English Camp. By July 1874 the last of the U.S. troops had left the American Camp. On September 6, 1966, Congress authorized $3,542,000 for the purchase of the park's site and the establishment of San Juan Island National Historic Park.

THE PIG WAR

Today, the events of the Pig War may seem like comic opera. At the time, they were deadly serious until talk replaced loaded cannon. It was Cutlar's shooting of the Hudson's Bay Company pig that caused the British authorities to threaten his arrest. Although he confessed to the shooting of the pig and offered to repay Charles Griffin, the Hudson's Bay Company Bellevue Farm manager, his offer was refused. In response to the arrest threats, the American settlers drew up a petition requesting U.S. military protection. With a zeal for glory, Brigadier General William S. Harney, the anti-British commander of the Department of Oregon, ordered Captain George E. Pickett (of Gettysburg's Pickett's Charge) and his Company D of the U.S. Ninth Infantry to land on the island. A forty-year army veteran and renowned Indian fighter, Harney was headstrong and cantankerous by nature. He decided the British government had wrongfully assumed jurisdiction over a disputed territory. To even the score, he ordered Pickett and his troops from Fort

Bellingham to occupy the island and "protect" U.S. citizens from "Northern Indians," not to mention the Hudson's Bay Company.

James Douglas, governor of the new Crown Colony of British Columbia, was angered at the American soldiers' presence on the island, and in late July 1859 he ordered three British warships under Captain Geoffrey Hornby to dislodge Pickett but with instructions to avoid an armed conflict if possible. Pickett, although overwhelmingly outnumbered, refused to withdraw. Upon hearing of the situation, Admiral Robert L. Baynes, commander of the British naval forces in the Pacific, advised Douglas that he would not "involve two great nations in a war over a squabble over a pig."

When hostilities were at their peak in August 1859, Americans under Pickett numbered 461 troops, protected by fourteen cannon and an earthen redoubt. Opposing were five British warships mounting 167 guns and carrying 2,140 troops, including Royal Marines, artillerymen, sappers, and miners.

Alarmed by the prospects that Cutlar's actions had prompted such an international crisis, President James Buchanan sent General Winfield Scott, commanding general of the U.S. Army, to investigate and to try to resolve the affair. Scott and Douglas, through correspondence, arranged for withdrawal of reinforcements, leaving the island to a single company of U.S. soldiers and a single warship anchored in Griffin Bay. Unbeknownst to Scott and Douglas, the governments in mid-September agreed to a joint military occupation until a final settlement could be reached. Harney was officially rebuked and afterwards reassigned for letting the situation get so out of hand.

4a American Camp

On July 27, 1859, Pickett landed and established his camp on the southern side of the island to the west of Old Town Lagoon on Griffin Bay, near the Hudson's Bay Company Bellevue farm. After enduring two storms at Spring Camp and wishing to move out of British warship's gun range, on August 22 the camp was relocated to a wooded area just over the hill from the farm. The post began as a collection of buildings from Fort Bellingham and conical Sibley tents shipped from Fort Steilacoom. Congress never appropriated funds for repairs or improvements during the post's fourteen-

4a American Camp

year existence. In contrast with the solidly built British encampment, by 1867 the American buildings built of green lumber were run down. The camp commander pleaded for money for a new barracks roof, saying, "it has become rotten—almost uninhabitable, and irreparable." One commander was "compelled to allow . . . stable hands (to sleep) in the stables." The Secretary of War denied all requests for improvements.

LAUNDRESS QUARTERS

The Laundress Quarters is a small, one-story wood-frame building with board-and-batten siding and a central fireplace that once housed as many as three post families. Laundresses were officially attached to the post and, like soldiers, were subject to the Articles of War. They normally earned a dollar per head per month usually doing wash for about twenty soldiers. A laundress had to be married and if she lost a husband, she had sixty days to find another or would be escorted off the post. While some laundresses ran through several husbands, more typically they were married to sergeants and maintained stable households. One laundress, Catherine McGarey, eventually staked a claim and settled on the island.

OFFICERS' QUARTERS

The attractive one-story wood-frame quarters facing the picket-enclosed parade grounds and flagpole is one of the American Camp's two surviving structures. Built in 1860 by George Pickett on his second tour of San Juan Island, the building served as a duplex throughout its military history, shared by the camp commander and his second-in-command. The plank-sided building had two brick fireplaces and chimneys. A wide porch extended from the building on three sides; lattice panels were placed between supporting columns at the house's ends.

REDOUBT

The contours of the Redoubt, an earthen gun emplacement, are visible on the hill to the east of the parade grounds. There are five earthen gun platforms constructed in the interior of the redoubt. These raised surfaces were timbered to accommodate eight 32-pound naval guns unloaded at South Beach from the steamer USS *Massachusetts* and manhandled up the hill. Only one gun was emplaced, and the only time it was fired was in honor of Lieutenant General Winfield Scott, who visited Griffin Bay on November 7, 1859.

The large boulder near the Redoubt is named for Henry Martyn Robert, who, as a young engineering officer, designed and supervised the construction of the Redoubt. Robert was two years out of West Point when he came here on August 22, 1859. After leaving two months later, he enjoyed a long career in the Corps of Engineers, retiring as its commanding general. He also wrote a little book on parliamentary procedure called *Robert's Rules of Order*.

4b English Camp

Shortly after the British and American governments confirmed a joint-occupancy agreement of the island, the commander of HMS *Satellite* responded to the American Camp on the southern end of the island by building a similar-sized post on Garrison Bay, about fifteen miles north. The British Marine Light Infantry contingent landed on March 21, 1860, carrying materials for the commissary building. Contemporary photographs and paintings show a compact camp of white-painted, one-story wood-frame buildings on a placid bay.

BARRACKS BUILDING

The barracks building is a reconstructed one-story wood-framed structure with a gabled, shingled roof. Approximately eighty by twenty feet in plan and ten feet eight inches to roof plate, the exterior walls are plank-beveled siding. Building access is by a single door on the northwest side and double-hung six-over-six light windows in the walls provided light and ventilation.

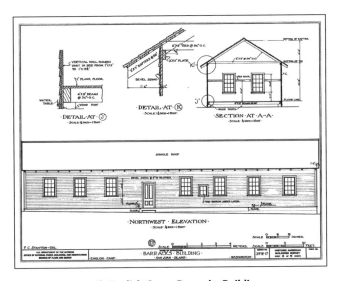

4b English Camp Barracks Building

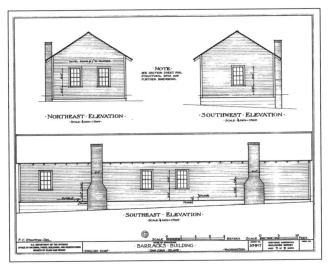

Two brick fireplaces warmed the building. A peg rack six feet above floor level on the interior walls was provided for the soldiers.

BLOCKHOUSE

The most prominent structure at the English Camp is the Blockhouse facing the Garrison Bay beach. Historians believe it is a copy of the fortification brought to the island by Captain George E. Pickett from Fort Bellingham in 1859. The restored structure of hand-hewn, mud-chinked logs ranging from five-and-a-half to fourteen inches in diameter has an exposed log base with saddle-notched corners seventeen feet square in plan. Entry to the first floor is from a cobblestone terrace through a vertically planked door. The building's distinctive profile is created by the eighteen-foot, nine-inch-square second floor placed over the first floor at a 45-degree angle, and a double-pitched roof. Framed in logs and clad with beveled wood siding, the upper floor is six feet high to a solid six-inch-thick log ceiling. Protection from all directions was provided by loop holes for rifle fire, cut into logs on each wall

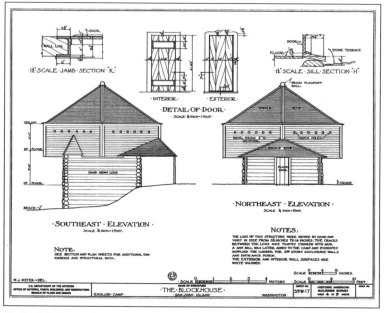

4b English Camp Blockhouse

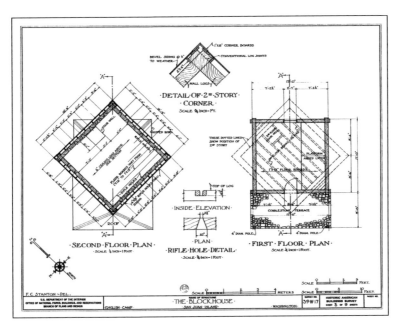

4b English Camp Blockhouse

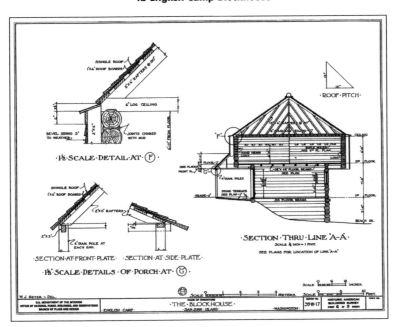

four feet three inches above floor level. The upper floor is essentially authentic, but because of tidal action, the log base has been replaced several times. A twelve-on-twelve pitch shingled roof is capped by a brass flagstaff ball.

FORGE

The Forge is a wall of rough-cut fieldstone approximately nine feet, four inches wide and high with a four-foot-square forge platform approximately one foot above grade. The fourteen-inch-thick wall is laid up with lime mortar. A brick-framed forge opening with a double-coursed brick arch provided access through the wall to the platform.

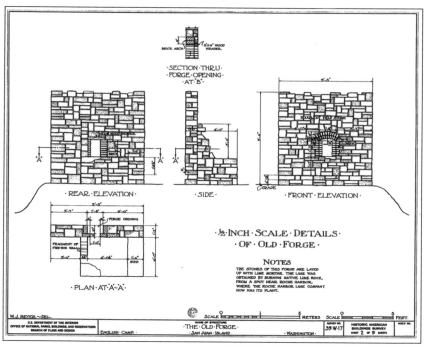

4b English Camp Forge

COMMISSARY/STOREHOUSE

The Commissary is a restoration of the Royal Marines's first building, constructed in 1860 as a storehouse to protect foodstuffs and other gear while the camp was under construction. In the early 1970s the National Park Service dismantled the forty-by-twenty-foot building and reused as many original boards as possible. The wood-frame building has a short projecting shed roof in one gable end and fixed windows.

HOSPITAL

The small one-story, wood-frame Hospital building is located across the parade ground directly behind the commissary. Similar to other buildings in the English Camp, it has exterior walls of beveled planks with a five-inch reveal and double-pitch gable roof.

FORMAL GARDEN

When Captain Delacombe arrived in 1867 as the English Camp's second commander, he decided to use the original vegetable garden site for a formal garden in the "Gardenesque" style developed in England in the early 1800s. The garden was a pleasant reminder of home for Mrs. Delacombe and served as a boundary between enlisted and officer territory. The current garden was constructed in 1972.

CROOK HOUSE

British immigrants William Crook and his family claimed a homestead near the English camp in 1876 and lived in several military buildings after the Royal Marines left. They built their own home in 1903, and the family occupied it until the last surviving child, Rhoda Crook Anderson, died in 1972. The Crooks and, especially, William's son Jim were influential in the survival of English Camp.

Index